EVERY THIRD
THOUGHT

Also by Robert McCrum

Fiction

In the Secret State
A Loss of Heart
The Fabulous Englishman
Mainland
The Psychological Moment
Suspicion

Non-fiction

My Year Off
The Story of English
(with William Cran and Robert MacNeil)
Wodehouse: A Life
Globish: How the English Language became the
World's Language

Children

The World Is a Banana
The Brontosaurus Birthday Cake

ROBERT McCRUM

ON LIFE, DEATH AND THE ENDGAME

EVERY THIRD THOUGHT

PICADOR

First published 2017 by Picador
an imprint of Pan Macmillan,
20 New Wharf Road, London N1 9RR
Associated companies throughout the world
www.panmacmillan.com

ISBN 978-1-5098-1528-9

1 3 5 7 9 8 6 4 2

A CIP catalogue record for this book is available from the British Library.

Typeset by Ellipsis, Glasgow
Printed and bound by CPI Group (UK) Ltd, Croydon, CR0 4YY

Visit **www.picador.com** to read more about all our books
and to buy them. You will also find features, author interviews and
news of any author events, and you can sign up for e-newsletters
so that you're always first to hear about our new releases.

For my daughters

Alice and Isobel

'Every third thought shall be my grave.'

William Shakespeare, *The Tempest*

Contents

Contents

Introduction

'Every day, you get older. Now that's a law.'

William Goldman,
Butch Cassidy & the Sundance Kid

No one will ever know exactly what happened inside my head on the night of 28 July 1995, but probably it went something like this. First, for reasons that remain mysterious, a surreptitious clot began to form in one of my cerebral arteries, cutting off the blood supply to part of the one organ in the body that, after the heart, is most greedy for blood. Eventually, perhaps some hours later, like a breaking dam, the clot burst into the right side of my brain, causing an uncontrolled 'bleed' that would achieve irreversible destruction of cerebral tissue deep inside my head, in the part of the cortex known as the basal ganglia.

My first reaction, when I came round in University College Hospital, drifting in and out of consciousness, was a kind of weird exhilaration. I had no idea about what had happened to me, but whatever it was, I seemed to have survived. Lying naked under a pink blanket in the intensive-care unit, wired up to the monitors, I was aware of being in the antechamber to the grave. Even now, years later, I can still recall the eerie fascination of this experience and of having, by great good fortune, returned to tell the tale.

Physically speaking, I'd been poleaxed. My left leg was paralysed, and my left arm hung from its socket like a dead rabbit; the left side of my face, which drooped badly for about ten days, felt frozen, as if my dentist had just given it a massive novocaine injection. I could not stand upright, or even think of getting out of bed; besides, my penis was attached to a Convene, a condom-like device that drained my urine into a plastic bag. My speech was slurred; every few hours, a team of three nurses would turn me over in bed, as if I was a slow-cooking roast. In place of pain – I was never in any pain – there was a hallucinatory sense of detachment, as if I was outside myself, looking in.

I felt then, and still feel some twenty-one years later, a powerful need to explore the consequences, and perhaps the meaning, of this very close call. In the words of the philosopher Wittgenstein, 'How small a thought it takes to make a life.' The event that I was learning to call 'my stroke' was an emergency that would not only transform my life, but also change my thoughts about death and dying for ever.

As the great American transcendentalist Henry Thoreau puts it: 'Things do not change. We change.'

1

A MATTER OF LIFE AND DEATH

'No man is an island, entire of itself; every man is
a piece of the Continent, a part of the main; if a
clod be washed away by the Sea, Europe is the less,
as well as if a Promontory were, as well as if a
Manor of thy friend's, or of thine own were; any
man's death diminishes me, because I am involved
in Mankind.'

John Donne, Meditation 17,
Devotions Upon Emergent Occasions

Ever since I fell dramatically ill one night in July 1995,
I have found myself in the shadow of death. From the
moment I woke on that distant summer morning, I have
been an involuntary citizen of a world I have had to
learn to live in, and be at peace with.

Thankfully, within a year,* I was on the road to some
kind of physical recovery. In my head I could never go
back to my old self. In darker moments, I would mourn

---

* See Robert McCrum, *My Year Off* (Picador & W.W. Norton),
1998.

a former life. Now, each day is a reminder of human frailty. Getting out of bed each morning will always seem like an in-house memo about my fate. How and when will it happen again? That's another mystery for which no one has a satisfactory answer.

As a lucky survivor, for more than twenty years, I've been living with the apprehension of mortality. To put this another way, at least half my adult life has been spent in the psychological equivalent of A&E. What follows is a book I don't have much choice about: it comes from the heart.

Matters of life and death are my special subject. As you will discover in the pages that follow, I have developed an affinity for conversations with brain specialists and their patients. My survival after 1995 has had this profound and long-lasting consequence with which I've had to come to terms: for better or worse, I am a lightning rod for the unwell. Strangers tell me about their sufferings and demons. But few things are ever quite as bad as we fear. This experience has introduced me to many sad cohorts of distress. It has also come with some rare blessings too.

On the dark side, however, you would have to be made of stone not to be moved by many stories from the front line of ill-health. Here is an extract from a letter I received soon after I came out of hospital in 1996: 'We, too, have become inhabitants of the world of pain. Our lovely daughter was diagnosed with leukemia. A year ago, she suffered a stroke, contracted a serious infection and died of pneumonia.' The letter goes on, 'Now we are living in hell . . . I feel that I'll never be happy again. There is nothing to look forward to.'

As a long-term convalescent, I habitually encounter people talking about their illnesses, their breakdowns, crises, and bereavements. Sometimes, a hurt shared becomes a wound soothed. Perhaps this runs in the family. My mother, Christine, a resilient eighty-something, is a seasoned Cambridge grief-counsellor. She specializes in collecting poetry and prose suitable for funerals.

Recently, I went to two burial services on successive mornings, and was reminded that, in my early sixties, I am no longer a spring chicken. Where strangers used to share their experiences of death and dying, now it's friends who confide their anxieties about the ageing process. Suddenly, everyone is having that 'third thought'. As one of my fellow mourners said, as she turned in greeting from the pew in front, 'It's funerals now, not weddings.'

To some baby-boomers, this is unwelcome news. Since the Second World War, biochemical research has excelled in defying the odds against us with discoveries like the structure of the 'double helix', DNA – the molecule of life. In so doing, medical science has sometimes seemed to persuade itself, and many of its patients, that our traditional encounter with decrepitude, infirmity and death can be almost indefinitely postponed.

At the same time, those post-war generations, in quest of self-fulfilment, have become complicit with a fantasy of immortality whose cruel outcome can sometimes be a yet more terrible endgame. The novelist Martin Amis once observed that, after the age of about sixty, whenever we think about the lives we have always taken for granted, we are obliged to concede that, in his words, 'This is not going to end well.'

Every Third Thought takes inspiration from my particular experience, but it's also a response to an immutable predicament. A self-assured generation, which has lived so well for so long, is having to come to terms with a complex but universal truth: make peace with death and dying, or find the inhibitions of everyday life in your final years becoming a special kind of torment.

The baby-boomers' response to this predicament (as one of them, I can recognize this) has been to put our heads on one side, look puzzled, drag on a cigarette, and say something like, 'We seem to have a bit of a problem.'

To which any rational person might respond: 'What sort of a problem?'

Baby-boomer: 'That's what we're working on.'

Rational Person: 'What, precisely, are you working on?'

BB: 'The problem.'

RP: 'The problem you can't begin to let yourself define or acknowledge?'

BB: 'I wouldn't put it like that.'

RP: 'Well – how would you put it?'

BB: 'Well – like I just said – that we do have a problem.'

RP: 'And so . . . ?'

BB: 'You have to admit, that's a start.'

Etc.

This book reminds anyone who has lived as if they were immortal that there are no privileges or exemptions – no backstage passes. The remorseless passage of time, and the unwelcome intrusion of physical frailty, must finally confront everyone with the same inevitable reckoning. The endgame is also about finding late-life criteria for day-to-day conduct, and becoming reconciled to the loss of early-life ambitions. You might feel thirty-five, but it makes sense to behave as if you are actually closer to seventy.

This 'Endgame' is rather like that award-winning feature film we've heard about by word of mouth. Our experience of it, before a final showing, occurs in the mundane sequence of trailers – episodes of sickness, infirmity and physical breakdown – released in advance of the main feature. However, after this Coming Shortly, we find our appetite for the movie falling off. In fact, we'd prefer to postpone it. Fat chance. Inexorably, when 'The Endgame' gets screened, we shall be in the audience.

So, welcome to my world. A word of warning: I am going to take you, the reader, on a journey down a one-way street towards an inevitable destination that remains as mysterious and terrifying as it is well known. To me, this juxtaposition of fear and familiarity, where life and death are braided together, is in the nature of being. My personal history means that I see the skull beneath the skin and the encroachments of oblivion. This is not macabre. I am at peace with any expression of this fundamental truth: the human animal, uniquely, knows that it is born to age and die.

To elucidate this sometimes baffling mystery, I have turned to some favourite texts. In doing so, I acknowledge two things: first, that words, which can be so comforting, are rarely the equal of reality; but secondly, that language can build a bridge towards a better understanding of a fateful prospect. Or, to put this in grander terms, that culture can be the medium through which we become reconciled to the incipient darkness that crowds the margins of everyday life. Empathy might be one key to a necessary rapprochement with the terrors of imminent oblivion, just as personal candour will help to make peace with threats of extinction.

The human condition has proved strangely resistant to modification. Despite the extraordinary progress of medicine, especially in neurology, and despite the many safeguards we have built into the way we conduct our everyday lives, we are still in the timeless world of our ancestors. To the Anglo-Saxons who settled Britain during the fifth century AD, after the Roman legions had departed, life was characterized by their poets as a sparrow fluttering out of the storm into the brightly lit mead hall, circling through the laughter and smoke for a moment, before disappearing once more into the dark.

Sometimes, when I reflect on the vicissitudes of my adult life, I sense that darkness just beyond the window. Then I feel grateful to be still alive, in the warmth and light of summer, out of the storm, with just the first chill of autumn in the air to provoke a sense of excitement at the times to come. For many, these can be good years. The experience of crossing the frontier into those final decades can be liberating and uplifting, with the added thrill of a deadline. Sixty, they will say, is the new forty. Actually, sixty is still the old sixty.

In her essay 'Considering the Alternative', Nora Ephron acknowledges, with bracing realism, that 'it's sad to be over sixty. The long shadows are everywhere – friends dying and battling illness. A miasma of melancholy hangs there, forcing you to deal with the fact that your life, however happy and successful, has been full of disappointments and mistakes. There are dreams that are never quite going to come true, ambitions that will never quite be realized.'

It may not yet be the beginning of the end, but it's unquestionably the end of the beginning. 'Never send to know for whom the bell tolls,' wrote John Donne in his neglected masterpiece, *Devotions Upon Emergent Occasions*, 'it tolls for thee.'

An 'emergent occasion' can also be a memento mori, as I discovered on 27 June 2014.

2

INJURY TIME

'The boundaries which divide Life from Death are
at best shadowy and vague. Who shall say where
the one ends, and where the other begins?'

Edgar Allan Poe, *The Premature Burial*

It was a fine summer's day in London when I tripped
and fell while crossing the uneven pavement outside
a row of shops – an antiques store, a hairdresser, and a
twenty-four-hour grocery – in Notting Hill. At one-
thirty on a Friday afternoon, I was leaving my weekly
session of Pilates/physiotherapy with Dreas Reyneke,
a retired dancer from the Ballet Rambert, a man of infinite sympathy, grace, and wisdom, renowned for his
healing ways. When I came out of his anonymous black
door, I was thinking about going home to shower and
change for a long drive to Devon, where I was due to
attend a wedding. Three steps later, I was pitched head-
long towards the opposite of joy.

The fall itself – my fall – occurred in an instant, but
also in a kind of slo-mo. That old weakness on my left
side, the residual deficit from my stroke's paralysis, had

long been a source of vulnerability, and now my worst fears from two decades were coming to pass. My first thought as I hit the kerb with my face was Tintin not Kierkegaard: '*Oh, *@?%$*!*' Then the menace kicked in: this was what people meant by 'a fall', an Anglo-Saxon word that's as old as the hills, rooted deep in our past, and edged with fear.

It's just a tumble to a child, or a pratfall to a clown, but falling is the curse of our later years, and a troubling one, too. The failure of the human frame, even in a fall, is a deep humiliation to our sense of ourselves. In the UK, per annum, about one in three people over the age of sixty-five will thereby break a leg, or a wrist, or, worst of all, a hip. (In America, the figure totals 350,000 per annum; in Britain, every minute, there will be six people over sixty-five suffering a fall.) That fall can be a gateway to incapacity and decrepitude: about 40 per cent of these fallers will end up in a nursing home; 20 per cent may never walk again. Among older people, according to Atul Gawande, in *Being Mortal*, the risk factors for falling already define our approaching infirmity: poor balance, dependence on prescription medication, and muscle weakness. 'Elderly people without these risk factors', says Gawande, 'have a 12 per cent chance of falling a year. Those with all three risk factors have almost a 100 per cent chance.'

In khaki shorts and scuffed trainers, it was not until I saw the blood splashed on the pavement as well as on my white T-shirt, and found its sinister metallic taste in my mouth, that I realized how badly I was bleeding from my head. Just a few days before my sixty-first birthday, here was I passing into a new world in which (as I lay full-length on the pavement) concerned passersby were bending over me with 'Are you all right?', and a smiley young West Indian woman on a quad bike was phoning for an ambulance.

'We're at the junction of Kensington Park Road and Pembridge Road . . .'

While she gave directions, I was groggily getting to my feet, and staunching the flow of blood, gingerly feeling the cuts on my forehead. Mixed with gratitude, my main reaction to this 'emergent occasion' was to be massively pissed off. I was bloody, bruised, and disoriented, but otherwise okay. Perhaps I was concussed, but I didn't think so.

My next thought was: *I do not want to go to hospital.* (I've seen enough of those, thank you.) *I want to go home.* But then the ambulance arrived, a pantechnicon of rescue, also in slow motion, lumbering into view like one of those cranky Red Cross vehicles from my Fifties childhood. While two paramedics began their first inspection, Time swept me forward on a tide of questions: Date of birth? Profession? Home address? Medical history? And of course they wanted to take my blood pressure. Every medic in the world wants to take your blood pressure. For the record, after years of readings, I'm always Mr Normal: approximately 125/80.

Now we were inside the ambulance, which was crazily tilted across the kerb, blue lights blinking, and they were radioing back to base about someone I really did not want to know about, 'a sixty-year-old man with head injuries . . .' Was that me? I could hardly believe it. But it was. 'Who,' I asked myself, 'who would have thought the old man had so much blood in him?'

My third thought, as the ambulance with its siren wailing began the short, almost stately, drive to St Mary's Paddington, was, 'This is injury time,' an inevitable prelude to the last exit. By accident, by chance, without warning, and when we least expect it, in a blink between opening a simple black door, and taking three steps into a summer afternoon: *This is how we go.* Here I was in this NHS ambulance, with old memories roaring into consciousness after a sleep of many years – involuntary panic; helpless weeping; primitive fears on the warpath; and the sense of life itself hanging by a thread.

Almost twenty years, in fact. Suddenly, I was back in that Islington street on 29 July 1995, taking the emergency route to University College Hospital on the edge of old Bloomsbury. That was on the summer evening of another fine day, and I was just forty-two, speechless and immobilized in the dramatic aftermath of a 'right hemisphere haemorrhagic infarct' (a stroke). I can recall looking through the window of another ambulance to watch the weekend world outside: shoppers crowding; cars inching through traffic; people with pints standing outside pubs.

That was the day I should have died, but didn't. Since then, a fortunate convalescent, I had lived from day to day as if nothing had changed. Call it *carpe diem*, or call it denial. In the back of my mind, I always knew there had to be a reckoning. Now, seated in another emergency vehicle, that moment had arrived. I had fallen off my perch.

Such a fall is a kind of failure, and an intimation of that final and bigger crash. As the ambulance, moving at an almost reckless 30 mph, turned into St Mary's, the paramedics renewed my passport to infirmity by asking if I could walk into A&E, or 'would you prefer a wheelchair?' Would I, hell! This Friday afternoon was becoming a civil war between two kinds of self, the proud vs. the vulnerable. From twenty years' experience, I was reluctantly being reminded of something I had come to know so well: we live in our bodies.

As I made my way down a long linoleum passage to check in with A&E, as if at a Holiday Inn, the dizziness and disorientation were wearing off. Exercise – in medical jargon, 'ambulation' – is rejuvenating. I was beginning to feel better. All I had to do was wait. As I sat in the waiting-room, it struck me for the first time that, with the *coup de vieux* of ageing, much of the adjustment we make has to do with accepting a walk-on part in a Samuel Beckett play, *Endgame* perhaps, or *Waiting for Godot*.

> Vladimir: Well? Shall we go?
> Estragon: Yes, let's go.
> *[They do not move.]*

☽

Contemplate yourself in A&E, and you quickly encounter some alarming 'What Ifs?', scaly creatures with merciless, predatory expressions, hot from the hinterland of your worst nightmares. What if my fall had resulted in concussion, or worse, brain damage? What if it indicated a more sinister problem? What if I was no longer immune, as hitherto, to neuro-degenerative side-effects? What if I was not discharged? What if . . . ?

In the universal predicament of waiting, one instinctive response is to open a book and find an escape in another narrative. Such distractions are always a nice route to an alternative, and perhaps luckier, kind of self. In a hospital waiting room even a copy of *Hello!* magazine or the *National Geographic* will at least pass the time. St Mary's A&E, however, offered not so much as a pre-natal pamphlet or a National Health Service handout to read. After my fall, I had no book to hand; anyway, I had lost my reading glasses in the drama of getting off the pavement in Kensington Park Road. Perhaps I should engage my fellow patients in conversation? It was back to Beckett again:

> Estragon: In the meantime, let us try and converse calmly, since we are incapable of keeping silent.
> Vladimir: You're right, we're inexhaustible.

As my equilibrium returned, I wondered how I might seem to the others waiting patiently next to me. As the victim of an assault? As a middle-class professional with an unexplained head-wound? A posh vagrant? We were a strange and ill-assorted bunch, rather less afflicted by the evidence of 'accident' or 'emergency' than you might imagine: an overweight Iranian businessman in a shiny suit, nervously engrossed with his BlackBerry; a pregnant woman and her mother, both in black; a small, ferrety, white-faced boy with his right hand wrapped in a dishcloth; and Brendan, a stage-Irish drunk, well known to the staff of St Mary's, who was now singing quietly to himself as he carefully removed his shoes and socks to inspect his very smelly feet.

> Vladimir: That's man all over for you, blaming on
> his boots, the faults of his feet.

Ever since, as a teenager, I first stumbled on the unforgettable opening line of *Murphy* ('The sun shone, having no alternative, on the nothing new'), Samuel Beckett has been a favourite writer. At this moment, in the aftermath of my fall, I knew that Beckett would become my guide to life in the foreseeable future, whatever that turned out to be. Words are still the best weapons with which to come to terms with ageing, and what Beckett calls 'failing better'.

It should be a peaceful kind of armistice. Why fight a losing battle? But words and culture – art, music, drama, and poetry – can make the difference. You need to know that this is my natural habitat. In the more than forty years since I left college, like the schoolmaster Holofernes in *Love's Labour's Lost*, I have eaten paper and drunk ink; at first, as the editor-in-chief of the publishers Faber & Faber from 1980 to 1996, and then as literary editor of *The Observer* from 1996 to 2012. In a privileged and fortunate career, books and print have been a guide, a consolation, and a *modus operandi*. For me, experience has often been refracted through novels, poems, and plays. Literature has filled a void, providing a narrative, in the words of Samuel Johnson, 'better to enjoy life, or better to endure it'.

Turn a page, and you find a new distraction, or another version of reality. Is this not the search for a fuller kind of experience? Art, which helps us focus on our quality of life, might also inspire a richer understanding of our mortal existence. I did not know it, but the first seeds of this enquiry, *Every Third Thought*, had already begun to take root in my imagination.

Here, at St Mary's, in the short run, the waiting was over. After scarcely a couple of tedious hours, my number came up and soon I was being admitted to the treatment zone. Next, I was lying in a private cubicle, behind a flimsy blue curtain, being examined by a very practical, friendly young doctor whose refreshingly down-to-earth approach was to offer a choice between a) a full scan and a battery of diagnostic tests, or b) a bandage for my head injuries (no stitches needed), some painkillers, and a taxi home. 'What you probably want,' she said, with a winning smile, 'is a nice hot shower.'

There's nothing so soothing as that old English cocktail of normality and no-fuss, also known as the sweet illusion of continuity. So of course I chose b), and went back to my regular life. By seven o'clock that evening, while the long summer day was still burning in the late-afternoon streets, I was back in my flat, and showering off the bitter aftertaste of A&E. But I didn't go to Zanna's wedding, and something had changed.

As Petruchio puts it in *The Taming of the Shrew*, 'Where is the life that late I led?' On this day, I had passed a fateful frontier of experience, and was no longer as blithe or as nonchalant as once I'd been. This afternoon of 27 June 2014 had witnessed a decisive personal transition: in this new world, where the endgame must be played out, nothing would ever seem quite the same again. I had survived my fall, and was still 100 per cent myself. And yet . . .

Together with the crossing of that immense psychological frontier – turning sixty – my own consciousness had experienced a subtle shift. Try as I might, I could not prevent another Shakespearean ear-worm ('Thus bad begins, and worse remains behind . . .') from burrowing into my imagination. Over the next two years, there would be more hospitals, more tests, more nurses, and, of course, a whole lot more waiting about. And all the while, my story continued to germinate.

> Vladimir: We have time to grow old. The air is full
> of our cries. But habit is a great deadener.

Actually, habit-the-deadener is a lifesaver. Since 2014, and during 2015/16, the year in which I have completed this book, there have been sudden deaths, irruptions of pain and loss, unanticipated afflictions, and the nagging intrusions of what I now think of as the 'third thought'. My fall had dumped me, metaphorically, outside an almost tangible, and imminently dreadful, threshold. Through a door, at the end of a sinister corridor of shadowy extent and mysterious atmosphere, is that a glittering and majestic jet-black arch from which there can be no turning away.

Perhaps, in the shower, I hoped to drown the apprehensions of old age. Yet, in some secret chamber of self-awareness, I was conscious that, like Prospero in *The Tempest*, I should now begin to acknowledge an inevitable rendezvous. Shakespeare's magician is talking about retirement, and I have no plans to retire, just yet, but the mood that governs his return to his dukedom is one that any sixty-something can relate to:

Go quick away: the story of my life
And the particular accidents gone by . . .
I'll bring to your ship, and so to Naples . . .
And then retire me to my Milan, where
Every third thought shall be my grave.

3

FOREVER YOUNG?

'I know death hath ten thousand several doors
For men to take their exits.'

John Webster,
The Duchess of Malfi, Act IV, scene 2

As I sit here now, putting these words onto a yellow legal pad, what I hear is the beat of my grandfather's eighteenth-century grandfather clock behind me, marking the seconds, minutes, and hours in the early morning light. In younger days, I was less a lark than an owl: now I'm always up with the sun.

There's no getting away from the tick-tock of biological life. In the words of the Psalms, 'The days of our years are threescore years and ten; and if by reason of strength they be fourscore years, yet is their strength labour and sorrow.' When I turned sixty in 2013, my first reaction was to fudge it. For about a year, I pretended I was fifty-nine or, if I could get away with it, fifty-seven. Secretly, I made a simple and sobering calculation on my iPhone of how long I'd got. Assuming about ten years left of my biblical span, just how many days, hours, and minutes remained? My score (give or take some leap years) looked something like this:

3,650 days

87,000 hours

5.25 million minutes

With that data in front of me, things seemed alarmingly finite. Look closer, if you want. Humanity has a clever way with the kind of introspection which might otherwise disable the will to live. It prefers to tell stories, at first through myth and religion, and lately through culture and psychoanalysis. Thus the bright, irrepressible dreams of youth morph into a more subtle communion with Time's reckoning, a roster of regrets which, in certain lights, can look like a catalogue of failure.

Most of these regrets are trivial (wishing I'd spent more time in the Australian outback; wondering about skiing the Alps, or trekking to the Forbidden City); some are sentimental expressions of wishful thinking (what if I'd stayed in Cambridge; what if I'd not at first married so young; what if I'd ever lived in New York; what if . . . ?). A few are more painful, sombre re-evaluations of personal shortcomings. In 'How Long Have I Got Left?', the *New York Times* article that inspired his memoir *When Breath Becomes Air*, Paul Kalanithi writes:

> The path forward would seem obvious, if only I knew how many months or years I had left. Tell me three months, I'd just spend time with family. Tell me one year, I'd have a plan (write that book). Give

me 10 years, I'd get back to treating diseases. The pedestrian truth that you live one day at a time didn't help: What was I supposed to do with that day?

Sitting alone with these words reinforces the isolation of the endgame, and its imperatives. So, back to reality. No time to waste. Towards the end of *Twelfth Night*, Feste reminds Malvolio that 'the whirligig of time brings in his revenges.' As these retributions begin to multiply, the mind cannot help but interact with the body. Both are doomed, the one trapped in the other.

There's nothing straightforward in the relationship a thoughtful person has with their Self, and especially with its human frame, in which body-image is just the most visible manifestation of that inner dialogue. Ageing only makes the dialogue more complex. How to shed early-life fantasies or mid-life anxieties, and acquire late-life wisdom? The frailty is all. Today, on the Tube, sitting opposite a full-colour reproduction of David Hockney's *Portrait of the Artist as an Old Man*, I was confronted with yet another fleeting reminder of Time's relentless passage, in the advertisements for his Tate retrospective. Throughout my childhood and adolescence, Hockney was this elfin, irrepressible presence, an Ariel of contemporary art. Now, plus a hearing-aid, he has joined the other ageing, greying figures of my youth.

With the onset of these later years, a process that starts at different times for different people, the fragile self finds that 'less is more', and learns to moderate its youthful egotism. Young people think they are immortal, and that the world revolves around them. Older people know they are mortal, that their future is not infinite, and also that they must take their place in the scheme of things. Among the important lessons about ageing is a new appreciation of simple pleasures: the joy of friendship and the satisfaction of small victories – an engagement fulfilled or a mundane task completed. Being alive in the world brings its own reward: the wind in your face on a blustery spring day, or the silver magic of summer moonlight.

From the many motivations for such a mood of acceptance, the most fundamental is physical. With the passage of time, the human frame slows down. On my visit to St Mary's Paddington, after my fall, I was forced to acknowledge this. Was I, for instance, the same person who had been wheeled, semi-conscious, into hospital in 1995?

Well, yes and no. For twenty years, thanks to a lucky spin of the genetic lottery, my recovery had been good. To outward appearance, I was comparatively unchanged. I would always walk with a mild limp, but my left arm (paralysed in 1995) was now, in physio-speak, quite 'useful'. Indeed, my physical strength, stimulated by whatever exercise I could manage, had probably increased.

Unlike many stroke sufferers, I had been able to return to work, in the competitive arena of the British media. Here, occasionally, conversation will sometimes default to questions of appearance more readily than to issues of press freedom. Last week, meeting J, an ex-BBC friend, after some years' hiatus, the dialogue went as follows:

Me: You look well.

J: Well, I still have hair, and so do you.

Me: Hair is what counts.

J: It's good to have hair after sixty.

Me: (*complicit*) Yours is white, too. That's so distinguished.

J: Hair is what really matters at our age. It makes all the difference.

Etc.

So much for the challenges of 'fake news' and the 24/7 media cycle.

Inwardly, however, I had begun to detect the first hints of a rallentando, a slight but (to me) perceptible loss of acceleration. Where once I could almost manage a semi-regular, stressful fifteen minutes of awkward running in the park, now I was happier to go for a swim, and become fishily at ease in the water in a way that was impossible on dry land. My daily coping strategies, perfected over many years to compensate for the various small physical deficits attributable to stroke, were no longer as effective as before. Perhaps most telling of all, in my imagination, I was no longer competing in my private 'Team test'.

This is the fantasy in which, even as a middle-aged man of sedentary habits and demeanour, you can watch TV and happily picture yourself participating in a national team at the highest level. In my case, until quite recently, I could watch a game of Test cricket, and (I know this is ludicrous) fantasize about bowling some brilliant reverse swing at a top Australian opening batsman. Or racing through the outfield to make an acrobatic catch just inside the boundary. Further back, in my thirties, in the same 'Team test', I might have imagined haring down the wing on a football pitch to make that brilliant pass from which Gary Lineker or Eric Cantona would conjure up another match-winning goal. Lately, however, even in fantasy-land, I have to concede an encroaching slowness hampering my career as either a Test cricketer or a Premier League footballer. In truth, I was always a spectator. Now, reluctantly, I am also a couch potato.

The strange and frustrating part of my condition is that I can easily imagine movement – running, say, or vigorous hiking – while being unable to execute even an approximation to a dash or a climb. Achingly, my body has wishes it cannot fulfil. In this state of frustration, a movie classic like *Singin' in the Rain* becomes a kind of torture, offering an invitation to the spontaneous thrill of a dance that I can neither accept nor even contemplate. When I watch those scenes with Gene Kelly, immobility feels like a prison.

These long-term inhibitions have trickled down into everyday life in ways I have come to accept. Compared to many stroke sufferers, I'm lucky. My walking disability is minor. I am still my old self, sort of. My progress is often slow and can be laborious, but I'm independent. Lately, I find that in crowds, at airports and train stations, I prefer to use a cane.

The upshot is that even the smallest journey each day has to be planned in advance. If I drive to the shops for milk or bread, shall I also go to the bank? Can I park close enough to Barclays to be able to cross the road to Sainsbury's afterwards? If I arrange to meet a friend in the West End can I drive to the rendezvous, or shall I find a 'Disabled' parking bay and take a bus or taxi for the last mile? What if it's raining? How will I get back? How congested will the traffic be? On and on it goes: every day becomes an accumulation of a thousand internal transactions in which nothing can be taken for granted.

☽

As the prisoner of my body, I have learned to subordinate rage to acquiescence. My strategy has become the negotiation of a discreet reconciliation – with myself. At the same time, there's our old bio-chemical make-up which is, inexorably, against us. When we, with our Stone Age brains, start to think about our mortal selves in relation to our ceaseless consciousness, and ask questions about the interplay between our physical well-being and our psychic equilibrium, we talk about mind over matter, but what does that mean, in practice?

For the last twenty years, I have invested my energy in the kind of optimism that sometimes masquerades as stoicism, pretending that I had come through a life-threatening passage of ill-health unscathed. Defying gravity, I have wanted to remain, in the words of the song, 'Forever Young'.

No one ever seriously challenged that fantasy. I found the wider world complicit with my dreams of eternal youth. Capitalism, by which we live and work, is all about aspiration, growth and vigour, ambition and success (even when the small print tells us that the price of shares can go down as well as up). Western medicine and medical practices reflect those values. The doctor's contract with the patient is to diagnose, treat, and cure – and then to send you, the patient, back into the world of the well, restored, renewed, and ready for the fray.

Agreed: the fantasy of youth might be my weakness, but it's also endemic to our society. The young, the backbone of armies throughout history, are also the foot-soldiers of capitalism, and they celebrate well-ness in thousands of intangible and influential ways that add up to a bigger picture of a world in which medicine must always make us better, where life expectancy is going up, and where – with a nip here, a tuck there, anon another rinse – the effects of ageing can be indefinitely postponed.

By chance, my own genetic make-up conspires to validate this fantasy. As if fulfilling some Faustian pact, my photograph over twenty-something years still betrays surprisingly little evidence of wear and tear (a source of irritation to friends and family who refer, darkly, to 'the portrait in the attic'). Well, 'Forever Young' might be the song that Dorian Gray hums to himself, slipping carefree down the boulevard, but it remains a tune fraught with irony.

When you are young, you ask, 'Who am I?' With the passage of time, that question morphs into: 'How, when, and where am I going?' That's an internal debate which can quickly tumble towards a sense of humiliation at the loss of 'fitness', provoking many questions.

One of the things about ageing that no one talks

about openly, or at best in whispers, is shame, the mortification of being 'unfit'. It's so fundamental that we learn to disguise it. After my fall, I made light of it to friends, and went to some lengths to distract attention from my cuts and bruises. Shame in older people manifests itself as defiance, intolerance, even rage ('against the dying of the light') and finally, with luck, a kind of ludic irresponsibility which, in the lives of some old people, can show as an expression of joy.

Nora Ephron, who compressed more wisdom on the endgame in the twelve pages of 'Considering the Alternative' than many weightier volumes, refers to Alice B. Toklas' famously blunt question to Gertrude Stein ('What is the answer?') as Stein was dying.

'What is the question?' was Stein's gnomic reply. To which Ephron's response is a witty riff on the possibilities:

> Do you live every day as if it's your last, or do you save your money on the chance you'll live twenty more years? Is life too short or is it going to be too long? Do you work as hard as you can, or do you slow down to smell the roses? And where do carbohydrates fit into all this? And what about chocolate? There's a question for you, Gertrude Stein – what about chocolate?

Eventually, in the small hours, at the dead of night, a darker strand in this line of questioning begins to plumb anxieties about things left undone (relationships broken beyond repair; feelings exploited; family neglected; friendships taken for granted; trust betrayed) and things not achieved, hopes unfulfilled (the novel I once had in mind; those plans for a cutting-edge arts centre in Northern Ireland). In the booming and shadowy mansion of deep regret, this opens another door into a multi-mirrored chamber of despair.

Here my reflections become mocking, even merciless: you are mediocre, ordinary, and insignificant, a preposterous bag of air. The disabilities you go on about are a physical manifestation of your moral and intellectual weakness. What on earth are you playing at? Even to write those words is to project an air of undeserved consequence. Vanity is the deadliest of sins, especially in the arts. The creative life, in all media, flirts with and feeds on vanity. It's the rocket fuel that propels the self into action, but also the firewall that inhibits self-examination, self-scrutiny, candour, etc. Kipling writes of his 'six honest serving men' (who had taught him 'all he knew'):

Their names are What and Why and When
And How and Where and Who.

The scrutiny of these 'serving men' is indispensable to a successful endgame. In the aftermath of my fall in 2014, 'Forever Young' insisted that there should be no scars, and that my body should not let me down. This was almost certainly deluded. Frankly, I'm not what I was, and it's beginning to prey on my mind. My inventory of dissolution, north to south, goes something like this.

At least, looking on the bright side, my hair is only hinting at grey. In the right kind of light, it can look dark and, on a good day, even lustrous. Elsewhere, other exterior parts have become vulnerable to inexplicable moles and growths. So far, on closer examination, these have turned out to be benign. Venture into the interior, however, and there's trouble brewing: my teeth need regular maintenance, and I'm getting long in the tooth – with receding gums that are prone to bleed. I cannot see this computer in front of me without reading glasses.

Further down, my chest will intermittently be seared with heartburn. There's an inexorable sagging of the pectorals and a thickening of the waist. If I stop to think about it, I feel bad about my bum. From the stroke, my left arm and hand have intractable 'deficits' which means that I am typing these words with a super-dexterous right hand. Both knees are crocked, my left leg is semi-paralysed (more 'deficits' there), and both feet, from soles to ankles, have the tingling pins-and-needles sensation of peripheral neuropathy.

This kind of ageing only exacerbates our consciousness of who we are, provoking new ambitions for what we might achieve, because ageing also provides a constant reminder of term limits. As an optimist, I believe this does not have to be a source of regret. Every writer knows that there is nothing like a deadline to galvanize the creative economy. New ideas flourish *in extremis*. 'Depend upon it, sir,' declared Dr Johnson, 'when a man knows he is to be hanged in a fortnight, it concentrates his mind wonderfully.'

In other words, it's all about me, and you, and the vulnerable self.

4

I – ME – MINE

I me mine, I me mine
All through the night, I me mine

The Beatles (George Harrison)

After the 1960s, the unfettered, post-war self found popular expression in many unconscious ways: in song ('I Me Mine'); in books (*The Selfish Gene*); and in society (the 'Me Generation'). By the millennium, this noble self was being boosted by fantasies of medically engineered immortality (consider Kazuo Ishiguro's *Never Let Me Go*). Today, in the global marketplace of free expression, there are more versions of the liberated self available than ever before. As Gawande writes, 'the lines of power between the generations have been renegotiated.' Lately, the older citizen has not so much lost status and control as begun increasingly to share it. Since the Sixties, the respect traditionally paid to the elders of society has been eroded, but it has not been replaced by 'the veneration of youth', says Gawande. 'It's been replaced by the veneration of the independent self.'

In 1946, once the baby-boom was under way, the veneration of the self acquired a canonical text: a popular guide to child-rearing and childhood, which appeared in post-war America and austerity Britain to influence our beginnings. *The Common Sense Book of Baby and Child Care* by Dr Benjamin Spock shaped the new generation and became the seventh-best selling book of all time.

As those first post-war babies came to maturity, another genre emerged to guide the successful and liberated adult towards a greater fulfilment than anything ever enjoyed by their parents. Women especially no longer wanted to be relegated to the kitchen or the bedroom. They began to read *The Feminine Mystique* by Betty Friedan; then later, *The Female Eunuch* by Germaine Greer; and possibly, later still, *The Beauty Myth* by Naomi Wolf.

For both sexes, these books had popular antecedents in bestselling psychoanalytic theory. Erik Erikson, in *Identity: Youth and Crisis* (1968), was among the first to describe an 'identity crisis' among post-war American men. This, argued Erikson, was attributable to a lack of creative work. Lives of quiet desperation were no longer acceptable for the Spock generation, raised to inherit the earth.

The central feature of Spock's advice was that he used the insights of Freudian psychology as a key to parenting. He taught, persuasively, that every child is a growing individual whose needs and desires had to be recognized and met. Several decades on, the voice that rocked the cradle all those years ago still shapes our consciousness. We remain heavily invested in notions of 'personal growth', with manic self-fulfilment now becoming a fundamental goal for an ageing population. Nora Ephron has fun with this obsession:

> We are a generation that has learned to believe we can do something about almost everything. We are active – hell, we are proactive. We are positive thinkers. We have the power. We will take any suggestion seriously. If a pill will help, we will take it. If being in the Zone will help, we will enter the Zone . . . we will scan ourselves to find whatever can be nipped in the bud. We are in control. Behind the wheel. On the cutting edge. We make lists. We seek out the options. We surf the net.

For successive generations, in the coming decades, the translation of 'the independent self' into a dynamic, confident, and purposeful individual will continue to be the will-o'-the-wisp of a happy retirement. The beneficiaries of Spock will continue to pursue personal fulfilment. But when modern medical practice becomes complicit with this quest, the conflict between the desire to remain active and independent, on the one hand, and the biological imperatives of ageing, on the other, is in danger of becoming another kind of burden for the old. Happiness can no longer be John Lennon's 'warm gun', but a more sensible rapprochement between the instincts of early life ambition, and late-life reality.

For some old people, such speculations are just that: theories. We have to recognize that in every geriatric circle there will be a few with an inexhaustible appetite for life. I think of Margy, my mother's neighbour, a redoubtable woman in her nineties who conducts her life like someone half her age. Margy says, 'I know I am falling behind a bit. I cannot catch up with modern technology. I do not climb stepladders easily. I wish I could wear pretty shoes, but comfort trumps style, so I just put on my bright lipstick and head out the door.'

Optimism will always be inhibited by biology. My friend the developmental biologist Jim Smith likes to describe his ageing mother's frank recognition of an awkward reality. Whenever she was wheeled off to hospital, Mrs Smith would croak, defiantly, on her exit, 'DNR! DNR!' (*Do Not Resuscitate*). In the Smith family, refreshingly, death was a subject for black comedy.

Baby-boomers are optimists who face an existential crisis. I know because I'm one of them. We have been overindulged with positive messages. For decades, we have had unqualified love and support. We never expected to face infirmity, or decline, or ... But now, suddenly, there's a list of afflictions with scary names that, after the age of about fifty, spring up like dragons' teeth: oesophageal cancer, varieties of leukaemia, coronary heart disease, etc. Today, as this cohort passes into history, it is a renewed awareness of the complexity of this final lap that's beginning to attract the attention of those who manage the third act of the human drama: accountants, geriatricians, and neurologists.

Ars vivendi, the art of living well, is a tradition that's undergoing a profound change. In the past, the common experience of everyday life was a three-act drama – beginning, becoming, and finally, leaving – in which the first two acts were all-consuming. In this new century, it's the third act that's attracting the biggest audiences. *Ars vivendi* is now matched by a new consciousness of *ars moriendi*, the art of dying or, to put it another way, our conduct of the endgame.

☽

To embrace transience, and to recognize our insignificance, must offer the best chance for any reconciliation with Fate, and possibly some long-term happiness and fulfilment – the longing that troubles every generation.

For myself, all I can hope for is to have inspired Alice and Isobel – my beloved daughters, emissaries of the future – to laugh and cry at the same thing, and perhaps to have passed on something about sympathy, kindness, and hard work. In this mood, ageing is all about becoming reconciled to, and making friends with, nothingness, *sub specie aeternitatis*.

Beneath the eye of eternity, I am on the record, in various printings of *My Year Off*, as the celebrant of a marriage to Sarah Lyall, a union blessed with a happy childhood for our two children. Now, however, that story has a new twist: at the beginning of this, my third act, Sarah and I are living apart. She, no longer in the family home, is resident in New York City, and the girls come and go in my life as peripatetic Anglo-American teens.

The lost experiences of former loves cannot be taken away, any more than life itself can be unlived. There's this existential truth: you and I might want our stories to be written differently, but it's still our story, yours and mine, itself the sum of countless human trans-actions involving love and hate, fear and longing, pain and loss, anxiety, passion, risk and originality. Acknowledge this, perhaps, and you can begin to make peace with the worm of regret. For me, the bright hopes I expressed twenty years ago have matured into something I never expected. I live alone, making friends with solitude, writing these words in a blue dawn, and functioning outside the recognized circles of hearth and home, older and slower.

'Slowness' is a theme I first encountered during my convalescence in the autumn of 1995. It was something I celebrated, almost as an existential blessing, becoming friends with slowness, both as a concept and as a way of life. As mature adults we become accustomed to doing everything freely, and at will, often at speed, possibly multi-tasking. With ageing, we develop a more cautious, serial mentality ('I'll take this one step at a time'), and then we start to become dependent, needing help with more and more, taking charge of less and less. At first, it's digital technology and small print, but finally, we'll probably want assistance with even the simplest things, such as getting dressed and bathed.

The passage of time enforces a reminder of the things we may never do again. Less sport, certainly; fewer mountain hikes or cross-country walks, perhaps; and no more mad running. The romantic young man or woman in the flying scarf racing through an airport to the departure gate or the meeting-point becomes an almost exotic creature, driven by impulses we can recognize, but no longer feel in our bones. Perhaps with resignation, we learn to appreciate the things we can do, and the experiences that are still available to us. As Coriolanus says, 'There is a world elsewhere'. Indeed there is, and it's probably inside your head. It will be the sensitive and fragile brain that becomes the future vessel of hope and resilience.

These restrictions of personal freedom have sponsored some peculiar foibles. I have developed a minor obsession with the lottery of green traffic lights, and also the lucky number seven, my birth date. I recognize that these superstitions are linked to an apprehension of 'Fate'. Perhaps this was incipiently part of my temperament but, in the aftermath of dramatic ill-health, I have become inclined, in the evaluation of possible future outcomes, to expect the worst. This, too, becomes another justification for taking things slowly. Slowness equals deliberation, and deliberation has come to equal the avoidance of risk. Yet, in younger days, I was excited by the thrill of risk. Does this mean I am no longer myself? Looking back over twenty years, it's instructive to see how that 'insult to the brain' has shaped so much of my waking consciousness, conditioning it to slow down, to re-shape who I am.

Historically, the oldie turned to God in the search for fulfilment during his or her later years. Today, with the idea of God under assault from belligerent atheists and an indifferent majority of uncommitted agnostics, there's still a hunger for a dialogue with something bigger and richer than individualistic materialism. This expresses itself, in the West, in a widespread appetite for culture. The crowds who attend concerts, exhibitions, plays, and arts festivals include all sorts and ages, but the majority are over fifty. For every Harley-Davidson propped outside the marquee, there will be a dozen wheelchairs within.

The horses of the night ride hard. Time is always catching up. For better or worse, we find ourselves slowing down in the diminuendo of senescence. It's now that 'every third thought' becomes preoccupied with 'the grave'. To a generation which has enjoyed unprecedented personal autonomy and fulfilment, these 'third thoughts' are strange and disturbing. The question is no longer 'Who am I?' or 'What exciting new experience can I enjoy?' but 'How long have I got?' and 'What is my endgame?'

At some point in the ageing process, our thoughts become binary – nostalgic or fearful: either a stream-of-consciousness entertainment about that younger self, or a more urgent interrogation of likely future prospects. And why not? There are any number of gruesome routes to the grave, most of them obscure to us in the present. This becomes one of John Donne's themes in *Devotions upon Emergent Occasions*:

> We study health, and we deliberate upon our meats, and drink, and air, and exercises; and we hew, and we polish every stone, that goes to the building; and so our health is a long and regular work. But in a minute a Canon batters all, overthrows all, demolishes all; a Sickness unprevented for all our diligence, unsuspected for all our curiosity; nay,

undeserved, if we consider only disorders, summons us, seizes us, possesses us, destroys us in an instant.

Donne's words could have been written yesterday. Another certainty is that our destination will never vary.

☽

Faced with the onset of decline, I have inevitably become tempted to monitor subjective physical qualities such as balance, continence, and mobility. After the age of fifty-five, no one I know is immune to the fascination of self-scrutiny in the shower, a quasi-medical procedure than can morph into something broodingly existential. It's a sober prospect, to which my recent summer fall added several contingent elements of anxiety.

After that 'emergent occasion', once the bruises had faded and the cuts had healed, I was more or less myself again, though probably rather less than more. In this new and reflective mood, I was beginning to wonder about something I'd never explored before: a course of radical physiotherapy at the National Hospital. My internal dialogue went something like this:

Ageing Pessimist: 'Better do something, you old crock.'

Eternal Optimist: 'A few swims and I'll be fine.'

AP: 'You're getting stiff. What about your fitness? You need to loosen up.'

EO: 'What's the point? I had a brain attack, remember? Some of those pathways are dead.'

The Ageing Pessimist might find physiotherapy routines boring and frustrating, but he also knows that, in the mantra of the physio, 'if you don't use it, you'll lose it'. Besides, he has not lost his sense of curiosity about the interface of mind and body in the vogue concept of 'plasticity'.

AP: 'Surely you've heard about "plasticity"?'

EO: 'What's "plasticity"?'

AP: 'There's a lot of new evidence that cerebral pathways can regenerate.'

'Neuroplasticity', to give its full name, is the exciting discovery that has transformed neurological rehab. practices in the last twenty years. It replaces the traditional view that our brains are physiologically static, and describes a process of neurological adaptability – changes in neural pathways and synapses – in the circuits of the brain that can result in dramatic 'cortical re-mapping'. One high priest of this new orthodoxy is the Canadian Norman Doidge, whose bestselling book, *The Brain That Changes Itself*, is a landmark in discussions of neuroplasticity, promoting a now widely accepted phenomenon in the recovery from brain damage.

The discovery that the brain is not an immutable organ but responsive to therapeutic stimuli has inspired some exciting initiatives, including Headway, in East London, a charity whose online writing programme 'Who Are You Now?' encourages brain injury survivors to tell their stories. Such writing projects can restore confidence, overcome communication problems, and enable patients to rethink their lives. From my own experience, I know that giving yourself the chance to be more like your old self is a good first step towards a fuller recovery.

My decision to sign up for a programme of physiotherapy designed to stimulate plasticity was also driven by anxiety. That moment in June 2014 – my 'fall' – remained a piquant reminder of Time's revenges. Even mild chronic disability has a way of reducing the patient, and closing off potential avenues of exploration. Perhaps it was inevitable that I should make my way back to the place where I had been first treated all those years ago in the summer of 1995. In retrospect, the National Hospital for Neurology and Neurosurgery, in Queen Square, has become my *alma mater*. Whenever I see the trim navy-blue tracksuits of the physio staff, I get caught in the crossfire of old memories. Negotiating the threshold to the gloomy Victorian interior of 'the National' is a difficult step back in time, troubled by many mixed feelings.

One of the principal frustrations of physiotherapy, I've found, is that so few of the questions you are asked, as the patient, seem to connect to your immediate physical experience and needs. With such routine investigations as a standard (ten-scale) questionnaire designed to measure levels of pain or discomfort, I am inclined to deploy evasive strategies. The temptation to cheat and/or cover up becomes overwhelming. Usually, I come away from a physio session feeling looser – yes, of course – and fitter, but also – worse – mildly criminal.

At first, then, it was strange and unsettling on this chilly November morning to return to the world of neuro-rehab., where I would begin an intensive and experimental two-week course under the direction of Dr Nick Ward, a pioneer for whom 'plasticity' offers possibilities of dramatic functional improvement.

Today, on the first floor of the Albany wing in the National where, twenty years ago, I was wheeled in for physiotherapy with Sue Edwards, I found Kevin, the medical orderly from the 1990s, still in his navy-blue tracksuit, assisting a seriously disabled middle-aged stroke survivor. Kevin, a shy, good-natured Scot, had been present throughout my initial recovery. It was both comforting and slightly disturbing to find him still there. Twenty years on, his presence reminded me to acknowledge my convalescent status.

Now Kate, one of the senior physios, was taking me through the paperwork. Arms. Upper body. Spine. Core. Left side. Right side. Feet. Sensation. Balance. So it goes . . . It was frustrating to rehearse stuff that must be in my notes, that inches-thick file. Had no one had time to read it? Inevitably, this reminder renewed some old rage about my affliction. Again, there was a persistent conflict – I was glad to be asked about my condition, but simultaneously resentful. I lay on my back, on my front, and on my side, and tried to find a moment of Zen. But that was hard: there are too many ghosts.

After the induction procedures, Professor Ward and his expert physios subject their patients to a sustained programme of intensive physiotherapy – repetitive exercises involving the finely calibrated movement of a shoulder blade, wrist, or thigh. Their aim is to stimulate new pathways in the brain, to recover lost movement and to renew old mind–body connections. To recover even a tiny percentage of former skills is intensely thrilling. Stroke survivors get used to paralysed arms, legs that don't move, words that won't form, frozen hand gestures, and steps that fail. Ward's programme sponsors an exploration of ways in which to break down these chronic prohibitions.

In the generation since I had my 'brain attack', post-stroke treatment in the UK has undergone a revolution. It's now linked to the best and brightest technology in the world. Ever so slowly, the brain is yielding up its secrets. We now know more than ever before about how, where, and why, in the cortex such an attack occurred. In several cases of stroke, among the survivors, it's possible to treat the 'brain-attack' with drugs, and diminish its impact. In new stroke units, across Britain, it has become common practice to treat stroke sufferers with immediate physiotherapeutic programmes.

And yet? We are still left with the human condition. We might live longer, but we are not immortal, and we certainly lose cerebral autonomy during these last years. Which brings us back to that ageing brain. Whatever the benefits of neuroplasticity, the brain remains the scene of more crimes against well-being than any other part of the body, as well as doubling up as chief suspect in the diagnosis of medical mystery.

As the victim of a 'brain-attack', a cerebral mugging, I am still in thrall to the mystery of my assailant. From what dark corner did he or she emerge? Were they tall or short, desperate or casual? Who were they, and what were their motives? The fact that so much about the workings of the brain remains mysterious used to be a source of anxiety. Now I'm at peace with the enigma of the brain and its crime against my well-being. I survived, didn't I?

As I waited one day in the hospital elevator, I caught a glimpse of my reflection trapped between two mirrors. It seemed, at that moment, an apt summary of my insignificance. As patients, we sometimes feel as if we stand between neurological research on the one hand, and everyday consciousness on the other, with the image of a cerebral cure – better, an unequivocal explanation – regressing infinitely into the future. However much I want to acknowledge 'insignificance', at the same time I cannot abandon my quest for a better understanding of 'brain attack', and its impact on my story.

5

THE SKULL OF MAN

Brain (n.): The convoluted mass of nervous substance contained in the skull of man and other
vertebrates.

Oxford English Dictionary, 2nd edn

Scan my brain and you will find a fuzzy grey scar, the
size of a thumbnail, but shaped like a tiny parsnip,
indicating 'the lesion' in my cerebral cortex. On a
computer screen, brilliant technicolour fMRI scans of
the brain make an entrancing image, described by one
scornful neuroscientist of my acquaintance as 'neurological bling'. To such sceptics, the importance of fMRI
is often over-sold. Does a scan suggesting in which parts
of the brain a particular process occurs, they ask, tell us
very much about the true meaning of that mental process? In black and white, which is how such images,
transferred to ordinary computer screens, are often examined by consultants and their patients, the fMRI scan
is not quite so enthralling, though still fascinating. Is
that me? you think. Does that fuzzy scar represent the
catastrophe that changed my life for ever?

The brain is both banal and magical. In our prime, it weighs about 1.4kg, and looks like porridge. When the broadcaster Chris Tarrant suffered a stroke after a long-haul flight from the Far East, he became addicted to 'the wonders of this extraordinary machine in your head'. He described to me how he had been going to a neuropsychologist. 'One day she came in with this plastic model of a big, fat, crinkly, porridgy melon. And I went, "What!" I mean I had no idea. I did say, "Does this make you believe in God?" And she said, "No. But it does make you think."'

To the *Oxford English Dictionary*, the brain is the organ of soft nervous tissue 'contained in the skull of man and other vertebrates', which is fine, as far as it goes, but listen to the Norwegian writer Karl Ove Knausgaard, who, describing it as an object of surgery, captures the thrill of the brain:

A landscape opened up before me. I felt as if I were standing on the top of a mountain, gazing out over a plain, covered by long, meandering rivers. On the horizon, more mountains rose up, between them there were valleys and one of the valleys was covered by an enormous white glacier. Everything gleamed and glittered. It was as if I had been transported to another world, another part of the universe. One river was purple, the others were dark red, and the landscape they coursed through was full of strange, unfamiliar colors. But it was the glacier that held my gaze the longest. It lay like a plateau above the valley, sharply white, like mountain snow on a sunny day. Suddenly a wave of red rose up and washed across the white surface. I had never seen anything quite as beautiful, and when I straightened up and moved aside to make room for the doctor, for a moment my eyes were glazed with tears.

The living brain is an object of wonder and beauty, with a complexity which has always resisted a comprehensive description. Historically, awestruck by its mystery, we have approached the brain through analogy. Thus, in the ancient world, the brain was described by Aristotle as an organ for cooling the blood, and again, in the seventeenth century, by Descartes as a hydrostatic fountain (after the fountains of Versailles). The Victorians made a comparison with railway networks and, later, the telephone exchange. In our own time, we sometimes describe the brain's activities in terms of computer technology.

Whatever metaphor we choose, it can only be an approximation. The facts about the brain are dizzying. Andrew Lees, the neurologist who treated me in 1995, says that below the surface of the brain, there are the '100,000 million tiny nerve cells that make up the grey matter.' The neurons of this 'grey matter', according to Lees, 'form part of a kaleidoscopic Internet.' In an ordinary brain, for instance, there will be about twenty billion neurons and each of those neurons makes on average ten thousand connections *every nanosecond*. The extraordinary computational power of a healthy brain holds the key to our lives as human beings.

When you start to consider the brain's many functions, you would have to be made of marble not to become enthralled by its complexity. In the fascinated words of the twentieth-century physicist Richard Feynman, atoms in the brain

> can remember what was going on in my mind a year ago – a mind which has long since been replaced. To note that the thing I call my individuality is only a pattern or dance, *that* is what it means when one discovers how long it takes for the atoms of the brain to be replaced by other atoms. The atoms come into my brain, dance a dance, and then go out – there are always new atoms, but always doing the same dance, remembering what the dance was yesterday.

According to an old medical joke, the brain is the only part of the human body to have named itself. Each one of these extraordinary machines weighs less than a bag of flour, and you could hold it in your cupped hands with ease. To do this, neurologists will tell you, can be a most moving and extraordinary experience. That, perhaps, is because the brain is more than just an organ, more than your heart and your sight, or your sexuality and your instincts. It's you, in every sense of the word – your HQ, your top-secret communications centre, your mobility, language, memory, and true self.

Your brain is also your window on the world. Oscar Wilde once wrote:

> It is in the brain that everything takes place . . .
> It is in the brain that the poppy is red,
> That the apple is odorous,
> That the skylark sings.

The novelist Jeffrey Eugenides puts it more prosaically: 'Biology gives you a brain. Life turns it into a mind.' How and why this happens is what Francis Crick, co-author of the breakthrough research into the structure of DNA, called 'the hard problem'. It's at the intersection of mind and brain that, as mortals, we can – and often do – live in denial about our future, until the fantasy of immortality disintegrates.

☽

The tantalizing frontier between well-ness and ill-health is like Lewis Carroll's looking-glass. We can step into a nightmare at any moment. On 4 March 2016, I received this email from my friend Ana, a Spanish publisher, describing the shocking irruption of such a crisis in her life. 'I hope this email finds you well,' she began.

'These two past weeks', she continued, 'have been a little nightmarish for me, in fact rather verging on the surreal. In a span of six days my father had eye-surgery and both my mother and my husband had an "ictus".'

This 'ictus', I subsequently discovered, is the Spanish term for any kind of CVA or 'cerebro-vascular accident'. Ana's account continued:

'After leaving the hospital's neurology ward with my mother, only two days later I was going back in again with my husband! They are both now back at home and we can even joke about it, but it has been quite unbelievable . . . You know better than me.'

Ana admitted that she had been shocked by her family's brush with catastrophic neurological impairment. Most distressing for her was the experience of a neurological ward: 'The reality you face in hospital is seeing people who are much worse off, and the worst of all, who are alone, with no family to care for them.' Among those who are well, such stark reminders of the brain's basic functions are distressing. Strangely enough, in everyday life, we forget to make these connections, a response which becomes an ironic illustration of the brain's place at the centre of our selves: that we don't, and can't, understand how it works.

Ana's disturbing drama illustrates the tantalizing truth about the brain: it's a puzzle wrapped in a mystery inside an infinity of consciousness. Indeed, despite the many incredible advances in neurological research – the scanning, the mapping, and the high-tech cortical examinations – the brain remains, as another specialist once said to me, the dark side of the moon in contemporary medicine. The miracle of the brain continues to frustrate human efforts to elucidate its hidden pathways. The neuro-physician remains like a person shining a pocket flashlight into a darkened ballroom, hoping to pick out a single precious stone. At this mysterious intersection of mind and brain, here's one inexplicable bit of data. For twenty years, my sleep was dreamless, something I attributed to the events of July 1995. Lately, however, my dreams have come back. I have no idea what this means.

But I do know, from my own experience, that the cortex is a part of our anatomy most of us take for granted, until it malfunctions. Among older people, there are many ways the brain can fail – Alzheimer's, tumour, aneurysm, haemorrhage, Parkinson's, motor neurone disease, and so on – with many routes into the third act of life's drama afflicted by varieties of neurological impairment. The longer we live, it's the failure of the brain that most threatens the tranquillity of old age. At the same time, it's in the brain that most older people will conduct their continuing fight for a quality of life. This is a direct consequence of an evolution in the Western world's mortality patterns.

Life expectancy continues to improve. In 1776, the average American could expect to live for about thirty-five years. By 1900, this figure had risen to forty-seven years, and by the millennium it stood at seventy-seven. In 2013, according to some estimates, there were more than half a million people worldwide aged one hundred, a figure that's set to rise to one million by 2030. A few snapshots: in Britain, there are now more OAPs than children under sixteen; approximately two million of over-sixty-fives suffer from depression; and one-third of all old people can't cut their own toenails.

Historically, the world's population was pyramid-shaped, based on the numerical dominance of very young children. Now, in Britain and America, the predictions suggest that within thirty years, we shall have as many people over eighty as there are under five. Mankind is just not dying in the way, or at the rate, it used to do. Since 1950, the median age of the global adult has been somewhere in the twenties, a figure that has long been on an upward curve. But now, there's a new milestone. In 2017, according to the most reliable estimates, the world's median age will pass thirty, and is projected to rise to thirty-eight by 2050. In Britain during 2017, more people than ever before will turn seventy.

Associated with these statistics, there's a change coming in the 'dependency ratio', the number of dependants (retirees such as grandparents) relative to the number of working-age adults. Now that baby-boomers are ageing, 2017 will mark the moment at which the dependency ratio starts to rise again. An older world becomes a world worrying about imminent disruption and short-term instability. An older world is probably less interested than heretofore in climate change and population control.

Traditionally, in books such as *How We Die: Reflections on Life's Final Chapter* by Sherwin B. Nuland there were three main suspects in the demise of the elderly: cardiac arrest, cancer, and stroke. Cancer, the affliction that people euphemize as 'the Big C', and coronary heart failure are big killers; stroke remains an infinitely complex exit route. But the subject which has come to interest me the most is the one that's less often explored, the cerebral dimension of ageing, and the decline of those little grey cells more than the grim march of heart disease or cancer.

☽

In May 2016, the BBC reported the findings of an Alzheimer's Society survey: nearly two-thirds of people questioned were afraid that a diagnosis of 'dementia' would mean their life was over, while more than half of those seeking such a diagnosis had 'delayed going to their GP by at least a year.' Out of 2,000 adults, one in five feared losing their partner or friends if they were diagnosed with 'dementia', and almost half worried that people would think they were 'mad' if faced with such a diagnosis. The charity said these myths about dementia were stopping people from getting the best possible treatment and also preventing them from planning for the future. Such patients' anxiety is understandable. No one, in their right mind or otherwise, wants to be considered 'mad'.

How does medicine define 'mad'? There are few precise metrics, and there is a continuum of 'dementia' that ranges, in the vernacular, from 'dotty' to 'bonkers'. The report noted that common symptoms of dementia included: 'memory loss, especially problems remembering recent events such as messages; periods of mental confusion; difficulty finding the right words; difficulty with numbers or handling money in shops' and 'depression and changes in mood or personality'. You might conclude that, logging this checklist on a bad day, almost anyone could be convinced of incipient dementia. That, indeed, is part of the diagnostic problem.

The statistics for 'dementia' are that it afflicts approximately 850,000 people in the UK. Furthermore, according to the BBC, some additional 225,000 people will develop dementia in the coming year, which equals 'one every three minutes'. Consolingly, much of this new awareness of cerebral failure might be encompassed by the kind of absent-mindedness conveyed by 'dotty'. And yet, whether dotty or demented, our ageing population faces a whole new battery of challenges.

6

SILLY OF ME

'The Question therefore was not whether a Man would chuse to be always in the Prime of Youth, attended with Prosperity and Health; but how he would pass a perpetual Life under all the usual Disadvantages which Old Age brings along with it.'

Jonathan Swift, *Gulliver's Travels*

Sometimes the intimations of neurological breakdown are like the most insignificant of mundane clues to a vicious crime. Yesterday, at the beginning of the weekend, over dinner, Brian (an old friend, now in his mid-sixties) spoke eloquently and at length about *Photograph 51*, a new play by Anna Ziegler, starring Nicole Kidman, a biographical drama based on the troubled and controversial career of the X-ray crystallographer Rosalind Franklin.

The conversation at the table was lively and specific, eventually morphing into a discussion of what else was playing in the West End, mixed with some grumpy-old-man complaints about the decline of British theatre. Today, at lunch, Brian turned to me and said. 'Have you seen *Photograph 51?*' And then began to talk about it, in animated detail. With a rather queasy playfulness, not knowing quite how to respond, I reminded him that we had talked about both the play and Nicole Kidman's performance just the night before. 'Of course,' said Brian. 'Silly of me. So we did.' The conversation moved on, but there was a shadow of anxiety in my mind. Brian is precisely at the age when symptoms of early onset dementia first present themselves. He, predictably, seemed blissfully unaware of his condition.

The assault of old age on the brain can radically change the terms of the endgame: it will transform the physical encounter with ageing, death, and dying into a crisis of consciousness, and an attack on the Self. This is an unintended consequence of our post-war focus on Identity. When the novelist Stephen King was asked by the *New York Times* what he was most afraid of, his reply encapsulated some of our most vivid contemporary fears. He replied, in almost jocular terms: 'Everything? Death, but not even death so much as Alzheimer's, or premature senility. My idea of a horror movie is *Still Alice*. The things that scare me or interest me over the years are less drive-in-movie horror stuff, and more what you find in real life that scares the devil out of you.'

The self is a fragile vessel at the best of times, and (whatever else it might be) old age is no longer seen as 'the best of times', if it ever was. Ageing besets the self with many storms that – in youth and early middle age – amount to no more than the annoyance of bad weather, offering no serious threat. The onset of these disturbing new apprehensions is beginning to attract the attention of serious writers. In a classic of this genre, *Nothing To Be Frightened Of*, Julian Barnes writes:

> When, at the age of fifty-eight, I published a collection of short stories dealing with the less serene aspects of old age, I found myself being asked if I wasn't being premature in addressing such matters. When I showed the first fifty pages of this book to my close friend H., she asked, concernedly, 'Does it help?'

Once you turn sixty, 'the less serene aspects of old age' become steadily darkening clouds of anxiety. In particular, the fear of ceasing to be yourself flourishes in the cracks that open up in the texture of everyday life: unexpected hospital visits for minor ailments; funerals and memorial services; peculiar irruptions of pain and odd, inexplicable bodily crises. Mostly, these add up to episodes of memento mori, sharp but fleeting physical reminders. Occasionally a moment of mild forgetfulness, like Brian's, can sponsor darker anxieties about losing one's mind. An unanticipated memory loss can provoke that darkest fear of all, the terror of King Lear: the fear of losing reason, with the associated loss of identity.

> O let me not be mad, not mad, sweet heaven!
> Keep me in temper; I would not be mad!

☽

The speed of Lear's disintegration is horrifying, but all too plausible. Families caring for Alzheimer's sufferers will know the ferocity with which the affliction can strike, often after a long, slow gestation. Shakespeare conveys his understanding in a single speech in Act II, which begins, almost philosophically, in the king's consideration of routine welfare:

> Our basest beggars
> Are in the poorest thing superfluous.
> Allow not nature more than nature needs –
> Man's life is cheap as beast's.

Then, as dementia strikes, the king become almost inarticulate with rage, denouncing his daughters:

> No, you unnatural hags,
> I will have such revenges on you both
> That all the world shall – I will do such things –
> What they are, yet I know not, but they shall be
> The terrors of the earth . . .

Finally, the king recovers himself, before dissolving into terrified self-pity:

> You think I'll weep.
> No, I'll not weep. I have full cause of weeping
> But this heart shall break into a hundred
>   thousand flaws
> Or ere I'll weep. O Fool, I shall go mad!

After this, as the action of the play unfolds, Lear is represented, on stage, as virtually gibbering, until in Act IV, he becomes purged of his anger and appears in a kind of second childhood, festooned with wild flowers, and challenging imaginary wildlife. Nevertheless, he's still conscious of his old self and admits:

> Let me have surgeons;
> I am cut to the brains.

The failure of the synapses in the ageing brain have their correlative in society. Disconnections isolate us. A new generation (our kids, their kids, and their kids' kids) replace us. Friends and acquaintances die or lose their wits. We only meet at funerals. Connections fail. Retirement breaks links with reality, and with life. Retirees die premeturely. Companies go bust. Christmas parties no longer happen. Weekends get overshadowed by ill-health. Children grow up and move out. Things change, fail and decay. Social consciousness becomes more marginal. The ties that connect us to the mainland of humanity become looser and looser. Solitude begins to encroach more and more. In the end, perforce, a lot of elderly people will live in a state of enfeebled isolation. As King Lear says, towards the end:

> You must bear with me. Pray you now, forget and
> forgive. I am old and foolish.

Consider the curious and distressing case of the best-selling novelist Terry Pratchett. The author of the 'Discworld' books was an acclaimed popular entertainer with a devoted following of millions worldwide. As he approached the end of his fifties, he was blithely looking forward to his third act. As he put it himself, 'I'm sixty. That's supposed to be the new forty. The Baby Boomers are getting older, and will stay older for longer.' But then he began to notice that 'something was going wrong'. At this stage, Pratchett could not be more precise; besides, he was fearful. Things came to a head in the summer of 2007. His typing had been getting progressively worse and his spelling increasingly erratic.

At first, as Pratchett writes in *A Slip of the Keyboard*, published posthumously, his doctor tried to reassure him that he was simply ageing. Pratchett was not convinced, however, and asked for more tests. His deep, private instincts about his condition were confirmed. After he had been diagnosed with PCA (posterior cortical atrophy), a rare version of Alzheimer's that affects the back of the brain, Pratchett describes himself as enraged. 'I felt totally alone, with the world receding from me in every direction; you could have used my anger to weld steel.'

Pratchett, recovering his self-possession rather better than King Lear, now followed his diagnosis with some intensive research into his condition, to get the best possible treatment. By August 2008, he was joking to the *News of the World* that he didn't 'know anyone who has got better' from PCA, before sounding a darker key: his affliction was stripping away his humanity a little bit at a time 'so you hardly notice, and until you end up a vegetable.'

In these early stages, he retained quite a good quality of life. 'I can still work at home and control my environment,' he writes, 'and the rare variant of the disease is not yet a real burden. The novels turn up as they always have – only the typing is hard. There will now be a moment when the letter A, say, vanishes. It's as if the keyboard closes up and the letter A is not there any more. Then I'll blink a few times and concentrate and it comes back.'

PCA, writes Pratchett with ironic stoicism, slowly robs the patient of memory, visual acuity, and 'other things you didn't know you had until you miss them', finally leaving you – he claims, with defiance – 'more or less as fluent and coherent as you always have been.' As Pratchett expresses it, his active consciousness of brain failure was the most poignant aspect of his affliction. 'It was like I had two diseases,' he writes, 'one was Alzheimer's and the other was knowing I had Alzheimer's.'

The key issue here is that our ageing society has not yet come to terms with the shame and distress associated with madness. Pratchett was facing 'an unstoppable process of dying by degrees', from a condition with no cure, and so it was with remarkable courage that he used his celebrity to publicize the Alzheimer's Research Trust:

> It is a strange life when you 'come out'. People get embarrassed, lower their voices, get lost for words. Fifty per cent of Britons think there is a stigma surrounding dementia. Only twenty-five per cent think there is still a stigma associated with cancer . . . When you have cancer you are a brave battler against the disease, but dementia makes you feel quite alone.

Pratchett, who died in March 2015, was a brave witness. Madness, in King Lear's sense, remains a subject we are still squeamish about. Varieties of 'madness', though rarely identified as anything other than 'dottiness', can be found all over the English suburbs, and especially by the sea, in places with names like The Pines, Sunrise Care Home (for Senior Living), Tideway, etc.

In these 'homes', the residents are rather like the 'immortal' Struldbrugs on the island of Luggnagg in *Gulliver's Travels*, who can 'never amuse themselves with reading, because their Memory will not serve to carry them from the Beginning of a Sentence to the End.' By this defect, writes Swift, 'they are deprived of the only Entertainment whereof they might otherwise be capable.' Grimmer still, among this grey army of retirees, a growing minority will face the worst threat of all: the kind of dementia named after the German doctor who first identified it. Today, for the first time, Alzheimer's families are beginning to publicize the affliction as it affects them.

☽

Prunella Scales is a much-loved British actress, renowned for her role as Sibyl in *Fawlty Towers*, in which she played the long-suffering wife to a domestic lunatic. It's the tragic irony of her old age that, in her seventies, 'Pru' has succumbed to her own dementia.

Her husband Timothy West has spoken of his sadness over the 'gradual disappearance of the person [he] knew and loved.' According to *The Times*, West's coping strategy is all about living in the moment: 'If you live from day to day it's manageable. It's when you start thinking of the past and thinking, "Oh, what a shame she can't do that any more, she doesn't appreciate that any more and we can't talk about this any more," then it's sad.'

For West, the first clues were apparently trivial. West first noticed there was something not quite right with his wife about fifteen years ago when he watched her on stage. Although she did not struggle to remember her lines, he noticed that she was not entirely inside the character's head. He could 'see her thinking' about her acting. For some years, Pru was not given a diagnosis, but once she was, the couple felt it was important to go public.

'Not to do it would be dishonest,' West told *The Times*. 'Particularly if we're going to appear on television together,' he says. 'Enough people know about the condition to say, "Oh, why aren't they mentioning this?" I just thought it was unfair, stupid and dishonest not to keep people abreast of it.'

Terry Pratchett had come to the same conclusion. 'It seems to me', he wrote, towards the end, that 'there's hardly one family in this country that is not touched by the disease somehow.' Here, Pratchett addresses a vital theme of the ageing process: there are innumerable ways in which the brain can fail.

So I went to see the British neurologist Andrew Lees, who has devoted his professional life to extremes of cerebral breakdown, especially Alzheimer's and Parkinson's. Where brain surgeons wield the knife, Lees considers himself as a neurological Sherlock Holmes, a detective at a crime scene.

7

LOSING THE PLOT

'I feel loved, ignored, needed, and like a dying albatross – chained around each of the people who cares about me.'

Richard Taylor, *Alzheimer's from Inside Out*

I first met Lees as a stroke patient in Queen Square, during July 1995. We have since become friends. As I've got to know him, I've discovered a great doctor with an enthralling personal story – an associate and colleague of Oliver Sacks, a highly original writer, and a tireless investigator into the weirder recesses of the mind. In the quest for a cure to Parkinson's, for example, Andrew was the first to follow the author of *The Naked Lunch* William Burroughs' experiments with apomorphine, a non-narcotic derivative of morphine.

Lees, as a Burroughs aficionado, is always willing to take an unconventional diagnostic route in search of a cure. He says he learned 'to treat the person not the disease', and was never afraid to use literature to help with his enquiries. He is also excited by the potential of plasticity and stem cells. Lees reports that he is often asked about appropriate recipients for donations to neurology. 'I would always encourage stem-cell research,' he says. 'That's our best bet, especially for Parkinson's. We've done foetal implants and shown that they can work. Now we just need safe and reliable stem cells.'

Not content with referencing the work of Burroughs, Lees will tell you, en passant, that the Marcel Proust of *À la Recherche du Temps Perdu* is also a brilliant neurologist. Addressing the frailty of the human brain, Lees likes to quote 'Forgetfulness', a poem by the former American poet laureate Billy Collins, a description of the process that begins in middle age:

> The name of the author is the first to go,
> Followed obediently by the title, the plot,
> The heartbreaking conclusion, the entire novel . . .

Andrew Lees could hardly be plainer about Alzheimer's, though the smiling tranquillity of his demeanour takes the threat from his words. 'It's a plague,' he says equably, as I switch on my recorder, and settle into his narrow, brightly lit office. Still, his candour comes as a surprise. I have known him for twenty years in the context of post-stroke convalescence, but have only recently come to understand his pioneering role in raising public consciousness of Alzheimer's.

The statistics of this disease, for an ageing generation, are indeed horrifying. There are now, for example, more people in the United Kingdom with Alzheimer's than live in the city of Liverpool. Lees describes how the prevalence of this plague increases exponentially over the age of sixty, and is now poised to become the second leading cause of death after heart disease. Worse yet, six million inhabitants of the European Union and four million in the USA have Alzheimer's, figures that are projected to double by 2030. Even more dramatic, in Western Europe, 1.4 per cent of the population has dementia. 'Alzheimer's is everywhere,' he concludes.

With flowing white hair, and the unmarked features of a much younger man, sixty-something Professor Lees could safely audition for the role of a junior wizard. 'Like the police,' he jokes, 'we neurologists prefer our own company.' His habitual dress of dark suit, white shirt, and black tie also gives him the air of a graduate student awaiting a big interview. Lees occupies a cluttered but functional room in a nondescript building a few hundred yards up the street from the National Hospital in Queen Square, where his career as a neurologist began. The drabness of his surroundings conceals one remarkable aspect of his research into the mystery of the cortex: somewhere in the laboratories adjoining his office there's a collection of three thousand human brains pickled in formalin. These brains are his stock-in-trade. Lees tells me, quite matter-of-fact, while discussing Alzheimer's, that a definitive diagnosis of the disease can only be made by a post-mortem study of the cruel tangle of amyloid plaques in the brain. 'The only way to be sure,' he says, 'is after death. We've still got a long way to go in our research.' This is an understatement. Much of the most promising research, especially into the possibility of a 'synthetic hippocampus', has only been explored with rat brains. Almost everything about Alzheimer's seems to resist investigation, not least because we have not yet found an acceptable way to experiment on the human brain.

'Part of the trouble we have with Alzheimer's is that it's always a difficult diagnosis to make definitively,' says Lees. Now, more than ever, younger people in their forties and fifties are getting panicky about dementia. He notes that he's getting a lot of self-referring, middle-aged patients who demand to be seen by a neurologist. 'It's becoming quite an epidemic,' he says. The problem with this surge in anxiety about Alzheimer's is that, unlike Parkinson's, there's no bio-marker to confirm that an individual is unequivocally afflicted – or in the clear. A century since it was first discovered, Alzheimer's continues to baffle and frustrate neurologists.

When Dr Alois Alzheimer first identified this condition in the early 1900s, the post-mortem examination of Auguste Deter (who died aged fifty-six on 28 April 1906), revealed that her diseased brain had become small and shrivelled with deep fissures. The vandalism perpetrated by Alzheimer's on the 100,000 million tiny nerve cells that make up our 'grey matter' is both horrifying and horribly destructive. This network of neurons, which has been the basis of memory, habit, language, and, ultimately, human consequence, cannot survive the assault. Deep in the cortex, the seahorse-shaped part of the brain known as the hippocampus creates humanity by processing a myriad external sensations, creating memory. Without memory, the human animal becomes, quite simply, a brute beast deprived of character and personality.

Taking a global perspective, the World Health Organisation has declared that dementia should become a global public-health priority. This looks like a quixotic campaign. From 2000 to 2012, about 99 per cent of newly developed dementia drugs failed to pass their clinical trials. Not only is there no cure for Alzheimer's, there's none in prospect either.

Lees, the off-duty magician, with a penchant for the psychedelic, cherishes the unpredictability of his calling. Who else, for instance, would take pleasure in reporting, as he did in a recent issue of the magazine *Brain*, that when he first came to study at University College Hospital, one of his mentors recommended him to read *The Complete Stories of Sherlock Holmes*? Lees described how William Gowers liked to teach his pupils that Arthur Conan Doyle had not only specialized in neuro-degenerative diseases as a doctoral student, but also that Holmes' famous 'method' was one that the professional neurologist could profitably follow.

In neurology, Lees notes, the diagnosis should begin the moment a patient walks into the room, based on the observation of his or her speech, aspect, and gait. Lees himself will say that even the most advanced technology can never replace the powers of simple observation. A hospital, he remarks, 'is still a crime scene', where the finest minds are needed to solve its mysteries. The National Hospital in Queen Square, Lees reports, is 'my laboratory'. For twenty years, as an out-patient and stroke convalescent, I have been lucky enough to witness some of the work performed in this lab.

Today, as we talk about his work, Lees describes

how, as a younger man, he had developed the use of apomorphine through self-experimentation, inspired by Burroughs. 'It was with some trepidation,' he confesses, 'that I injected myself with 1mg of apomorphine as the prelude to a fuller clinical investigation.' As a result of his willingness to take such risks, apomorphine became licensed for routine treatment, with some remarkable results during the 1970s. Initially, this was the focus of Lees' research. He would not move into the grimmer world of Alzheimer's treatment until the 1980s and '90s. Today, he is one of its foremost specialists in the world.

☽

As a literary critic, I have occasionally speculated about 'the narrative gene' in our brains. How else to explain the human animal's timeless and universal fascination with 'story', or the importance of good storytelling in the conduct of culture, politics, and society? Today, I find that this special opportunity to discuss 'losing the plot' with Professor Lees stimulates my imaginative response to the tale he begins to tell, the experience of witnessing a human mind becoming progressively un-tethered from its reason. In fact, I'm riveted.

Lees starts, quite gently, with the mental slowing and inflexibility naturally associated with ageing. Cerebral atrophy, he tells me, will make the brain of some ninety-year-olds look like a shrivelled walnut, a quite tangible decline. A healthy adult in the prime of life has a brain that's like a balloon which has been crumpled up to be stuffed into the skull. The more evolved the mammal, the more convoluted the brain becomes. Very simple mammals have relatively smooth brains. Our brains are very convoluted. As we get older, the substance of the brain shrinks. Our increasing difficulties with decision-making in later life, the origin of a proverb like 'You can't teach an old dog new tricks', hold a special fascination for Lees. He is all too aware of the way in which the changes attributable to ageing contribute to the negative stereotype of the elderly as obstinate, selfish, infantile, incompetent, and crotchety, and adds that 'the saving grace of wisdom depends heavily on long-term memory'.

Here, he makes this prediction: 'As society's attitudes to Alzheimer's evolve and the threshold for diagnosis lowers, more and more people over the age of sixty will be asked a series of questions designed to probe their orientation in time and place, their short-term memory, and their language skills.' In the near future, then, we are likely to blame the qualities we associate with age less on the individual and more on the afflictions of dementia.

Once the difficult diagnosis of Alzheimer's has been made, the narrative of this disease defines one of the greatest scourges of the twenty-first century. This is a neuro-degenerative affliction that strips the patient of all the qualities we recognize as human. If that sounds like hyperbole, consider a typical account of the physical and mental trajectory experienced by an Alzheimer's sufferer. At first, invoking the language of the consulting-room or the lab, Lees describes the trajectory of

Alzheimer's as 'distressing'. When pressed, he concedes that it's 'scary'.

The poet W. H. Auden once compared Death to 'the rumble of distant thunder at a picnic'. The first three stages of Alzheimer's typically occur as darkening storm clouds forming, at first on a distant horizon, as it were, at the end of a perfect summer's day. Every sixty-something knows the thin line in mundane consciousness between accepting a measure of mild forgetfulness ('Now where did I put my car keys?'), and worrying about the darker significance of a more persistent memory loss. At a certain age, almost everyone will joke about 'losing the plot'. Many Alzheimer's patients, in their fifties and sixties, will be active and vigorous, successful citizens living full rich lives.

The initial symptoms – occasional flashes of anger, inexplicable forgetfulness – are so slight that many families will miss them, attributing sudden bouts of irrationality to the frustrating mystery of old age. As we have already seen in the case of Terry Pratchett, more alert and self-aware patients may sense that something is wrong, something that, at this stage, many outsiders, and even some doctors, might overlook.

The second phase in the progress of the illness becomes the unmistakable onset of memory loss: an inability to recognize acquaintances, or some repetitive questions in everyday conversation. Once again, the patient's friends and family may be inclined to attribute this to ageing – until it becomes clear that something terrible is happening to the patient's brain.

Finally, in the third stage of Alzheimer's, Lees says

that it becomes impossible to ignore the disintegration of the patient's mind. Mothers and fathers, uncles and grandparents, become palpably 'mad'. Now a full medical examination and diagnosis becomes inevitable. For families and loved ones, in particular, there can be no more denial. In the end, says Lees, 'you are no longer able to treat the patient. All you can do is do what you can to help their families.'

Sometimes, the brain can be strangely merciful. At this dreadful turning point, it is likely that when the patient is informed of his or her fate, they will no longer be competent to retain, or respond to, this information. As Lees puts it, 'Alzheimer's ignites in the hippocampus and the entorhinal cortex. Once these parts of the emotional brain have been burned down, there can be no more episodic memory.'

This terrible moment spells the end of an individual's character and personality. With episodic memory gone, past and present become for ever dissociated. A thousand daily functions – for example, knowing how to make a cup of tea, and remembering where to find, and how to use, milk and sugar – become impossible. Once episodic memory has gone, the Alzheimer's patient is at the mercy of cerebral Furies, a process that falls into further patterns of horrifying dehumanization. 'You have to ask yourself this question,' says Lees. 'Are we human without memory? Almost the only means of human communication at the end will be the comforts of touch, and perhaps some music.'

☽

Alzheimer's patients exhibit many responses to this 'silent plague'. First, there is incomprehension. This can sometimes be a comparatively benign state in which the patient becomes merely childlike. The novelist Iris Murdoch, who was finally diagnosed with Alzheimer's in 1997 (she died in 1999), would spend her days watching children's TV. Her husband, John Bayley, reported in his memoir, *Iris*, that his wife 'remains her old self in many ways'. He goes on:

> The power of concentration has gone, along with the ability to form coherent sentences, and to remember where she is, or has been. She does not know she has written twenty-seven remarkable novels . . . If an admirer asks her to sign a copy of one of her novels . . . it takes her some time, but the letters are still formed with care, and resemble, in a surreal way, her old handwriting. The old gentleness remains.

Once forgetfulness advances more completely, language itself becomes redundant and – without words – how can life have any meaning? At this point – this is the next stage – the patient might become disturbed and violent. Subsequently, as dementia takes hold, there will be a need for hospitalization, where possible. In some cases, there will have to be a referral to a nursing home for twenty-four-hour care.

Lees describes to me how, at the peak of his career, he would treat as many as a hundred dementia cases. Now he confines himself to just a handful of Alzheimer's patients. He observes, with sadness, how the disease takes its toll on everyone: spouses, families, children, and partners. There will be no respite. Typically, all involved will long for the death of the afflicted, but this may not occur for five, seven, even ten years. In this acute stage, the fate of the Alzheimer's sufferer is terrifying. The complete destruction of what Lees calls 'the emotional brain' may result in explosive rage, wild cravings for food, and a kind of manic fearlessness. Mixed in with an intolerable loss of social skills, there will be the almost total inability to recognize old friends and family, or recall past events. The annihilation of the self deprives the patient of all autonomy, reducing them to a sub-human husk.

For the care-givers, the devastation wrought by Alzheimer's is like a life sentence, in which every nuance of everyday life becomes a source of anxiety and pain. In *Iris*, John Bayley recalls 'a brisk exchange' with a fellow carer, a woman whose husband also has Alzheimer's. 'Like being chained to a corpse, isn't it?' says the woman cheerfully. 'A much-loved corpse naturally,' she amends, with an implicit suggestion that Bayley might be willing to abandon what he calls 'the usual proprieties that went with our situation'. Meanwhile, alone at home, there are precious few 'proprieties'. Bayley has to struggle to stay in touch with his 'lost' wife:

> Our mode of communication seems like underwater sonar, each bouncing pulsations off the other, and listening for an echo. The baffling moments at which I cannot understand what Iris is saying, or about whom or what . . . can sometimes be dispelled

by a jokey parody of helplessness, and trying to make it mutual. Both of us at a loss for words.

As well as the loss of language, there is the growing loss of affect, and facial expression. The Alzheimer face is often described as 'the lion face' – sombre, expressionless, and frozen in leonine impassivity, occasionally broken by a mad smile. Bayley, however, manages to find humanity and even fun in mundane tasks, like getting up in the morning. 'Dressing most days', he writes, 'is a reasonably happy and comic business. I am myself still far from sure which way her underpants are supposed to go: we usually decide between us that it doesn't matter . . . I ought to give her a bath, but I tend to postpone it from day to day.'

Bayley does his best, in his stoic English way, to put a brave face on things, but an inevitable bleakness creeps in: 'Most days are in fact for [Iris] a sort of despair, although despair suggests a conscious and positive state and this is a vacancy which frightens her by its lack of dimension.' Bayley tries to deal with the anxiety by suggesting a distraction like a shopping trip in the car. 'Something urgent, practical, giving the illusion of sense and routine.'

For the Alzheimer's nurse, there remains the consolation that their patients are usually oblivious to their condition. In the clinical atmosphere of the National, I am finding it hard to imagine such a state of mind, and Lees is trying to elucidate his experience for my benefit. Reflecting on this stage of the disease, he reports that 'some sufferers do remain conscious of their state, paradoxical as this seems. The torment of knowing that you cannot speak or think what you want must be intolerable, and I have met patients in whom such torment is clearly visible.' Discussing this unprecedented torture of the mind, Lees projects a kind of priest-like serenity that must, I speculate, have been a great comfort to his patients and, most especially, their carers.

Iris Murdoch, contrariwise, seems to have retained some sense of reality. When Bayley surrendered to his care-giver's compulsion to demonstrate how bad things were, his wife would surprise him. 'I made a savage comment today,' he writes, 'about the grimness of our outlook. Iris looks relieved and intelligent. She says: "But I love you."' Her husband fights with his rage ('I get Iris into a seat and give her a violent surreptitious punch on the arm'), and also with the torment that this brings:

> The exasperation of being followed about the house now by Iris is as strong and genuine as is my absolute need for it. Were she to avoid me, I would pursue her as anxiously, if not quite so obsessively, as she now pursues me.

Heartbreakingly, every now and then Iris would articulate her feeling that she was 'sailing into darkness'.

If he were a neurologist, Bayley concludes, he would find it hard to believe in such flashes of lucidity. 'The words which Iris used [as a novelist] with such naturalness and brilliance cannot be stacked there, silently, sending out an occasional signal. Or can they?' He notes that his wife's 'eerie felicities' are like the things a young child will come out with to delight and amuse parents and friends.

Finally, there is always Bayley's own terror of imminent mortality, a strange, sad coda to an infinitely sad and affecting memoir:

> What will [Iris] do if I die? If I'm ill and have to go to hospital; if I have to stay in bed – what will she do then? I make these demands with increasing hostility and violence. I am furious to see my words are getting nowhere, and yet relieved too by this, so that I can continue my fury.

Andrew Lees, musing now on a lifetime's experience of neuro-degenerative diseases, tells me that, as a doctor, he can never predict his patients' response to their plight. 'It's hard,' he concludes, 'not to present their predicament as anything but terribly bleak,' and yet there are occasional moments of humanity.

When former US president Ronald Reagan, who also suffered from Alzheimer's, first became conscious of his failing memory, he would cover up his forgetfulness with feeble jokes. Lees says such strategies are quite common, as a defence mechanism. 'Especially at the beginning, there's a lot of anxiety. But occasionally you'll find a quite different reaction.' He recalls a recent patient, a man in his sixties whom he described to me as 'a happy man'. At one consultation, to test his condition, Lees had asked the patient if he knew what day of the week it was.

'Why do you ask me that?' said the man, in a tone of puzzlement. 'At my age, the day of the week really does not matter. I'm retired. I walk the dog. I watch television. In the afternoon, I have a little sleep. Days of the week don't matter to me.'

To every question that Lees put to him, this man had 'a smart answer' of Zen-like equanimity. A bit later in the consultation Lees asked, 'Do you know where you are?' To which his patient cheerfully replied, 'I've no idea, but it doesn't matter. My wife brings me. She's here; she'll take me home. That's enough.' Lees can only laugh. 'His wife was sitting behind him, and she was almost beside herself. She'd had it up to here.' He shakes his head. 'In the end, it's the families that stop visiting. There's no point. It becomes too painful.'

With some regret, even dismay, Lees will concede how painfully slow the progress of neurological research has been throughout his career, noting that there are no good animal models available for research into neuro-degeneration. 'We still don't know if old primates can develop Alzheimer's,' he observes. 'We have to look at human tissue to try to understand what's going on in the brain, and we are making some progress with "brain-mapping", though that can be over-interpreted.'

Despite these caveats, he remains impressively optimistic about the prospects for neurology. 'Am I hopeful?' he asks, turning rhetorical. 'Yes – I believe we will know much more in the future. Is the brain complicated? Of course it is. But I believe in happy accidents. We always say we are "five years" from some important break-through. But it could happen now, tomorrow.' Lees wears the serene expression of a wizard who trusts his magic. 'We need blind luck – and prepared minds,' he concludes.

Lees himself seems to derive some of his impressive equanimity from the practice of mental and physical exercise, a vital element in keeping mind and body equally fit. There is, otherwise, no reliable treatment for neuro-degeneration. 'Age remains the major risk factor,' he says. 'Sixty-five,' he concludes, almost merrily, as a man in his sixties, 'is still the watershed in the diagnosis and treatment of Alzheimer's and Parkinson's.'

This fear of neuro-degeneration haunts the profession. The renowned neurosurgeon Henry Marsh is a former colleague of Lees', and equally well versed in the complexity of the cortex. The bestselling author of *Do No Harm* turned out to be impressively sanguine about brain surgery but – perhaps because he has spent a lifetime operating on diseased brains – profoundly apprehensive about his own neurological future prospects.

8

DO NO HARM

The brain is wider than the sky,
For, put them side by side,
The one the other will include
With ease, and you beside.

Emily Dickinson, *Complete Poems*, CXXVI

I first met Henry Marsh in the grounds of the Bishop's
Palace at the Wells Festival of Literature in October
2014. He had just published *Do No Harm: Stories of
Life, Death and Brain Surgery*, and I was due to interview him about it in front of an audience. I was looking
forward to this encounter, but I did not know quite
what to expect. By reputation, Marsh is a bit of a
maverick, an 'eminent brain surgeon', and Alpha male,
who used to bicycle to work without a safety helmet,
a free-thinker who is not afraid to speak his mind
about his disaffection with NHS bureaucracy, and also
the engaging subject of *Your Life in their Hands*, an
award-winning TV documentary about his work as a
charismatic surgeon which I had once watched on a
transatlantic flight.

Do No Harm, a title inspired by the Hippocratic oath, spoke directly to my fascination with the brain, but it was, on first reading, distinctly shocking. In twenty-five unsparing chapters, replete with gripping detail, Marsh takes the reader through the often bloody crises of brain surgery from Aneurysm to Oligodendroglioma ('a tumour of the central nervous system'). In the course of this journey, he exempts no one, least of all himself. 'How does it feel', he asks at the outset, 'to hold someone's life in your hands, to cut into the stuff that creates thought, feeling and reason?'

I had always known that brain surgeons are the sort of characters who relish the drama of the operating theatre. Their risk-taking, rock-star instincts are essential if they are to perform their often dangerous procedures. Here, on paper, was a senior member of his profession who not only celebrated, in blunt terms, the art of playing God, but who was also tormented by the cost of his life's work. 'How does it feel', he challenges himself, 'to perform a live-saving operation that goes badly wrong?' From the first page of *Do No Harm* (I soon got over my squeamishness), I was hooked, not least because Marsh exhibits a fearsome and exhilarating candour. 'Much of what happens in hospitals', he writes, 'is a matter of luck, both good and bad; success and failure are often out of the doctor's control.'

None of this prepared me for our first meeting, in a tent next to the main stage of the Wells Festival. Marsh was waiting there in his pin-stripe suit, but he was far from the ice-cool master of the scalpel. A newcomer to literary self-promotion, he was chatty, animated, and obviously nervous. My first job that afternoon was to reassure him that his book was compulsive reading (it was, indeed, about to become a bestseller), and also that every member of the sold-out audience was going to be on the edge of their seat.

The next hour flashed by. From the moment Marsh began to describe, in stomach-turning detail, what it's like to saw open a patient's skull before brain surgery, his audience of open-mouthed seniors was rapt. As blood and bone-matter spattered our conversation, my 'interview' became a formality. I threw away my well-rehearsed questions about 'consciousness', 'mind/body', and 'neuro-plasticity', and surrendered to the tales he was telling about the emergencies of his 'operating theatre'. Rarely had that arena seemed so dramatic or life-changing.

As we talked, during that weekend in Wells, I found Henry – as I now knew him – to be a passionate man who freely confided the romance of his younger days, the 'exquisite pleasures' of his early career in neuro-surgery, and 'the wonderful mystery' of the brain. Unlike some surgeons, he openly admitted deriving 'spiritual consolation' from Crick's 'hard problem', the infinite conundrum of human consciousness. 'The problem for neuroscience,' said Henry, 'is that we've never met a brain, apart from our own, and so we have to describe it by analogy.' Thus it was that the brain would be described by Descartes as a hydrostatic fountain.

The wonder of the brain is only equalled by its astounding role in the narrative of our humanity, and our life on earth. Considering the dazzling complexity of the organ, the idea that a brain surgeon must cut into thought itself, and through emotion and reason, is still mind-boggling. The idea that memories, dreams, and reflections should consist of jelly is beyond our ordinary comprehension.

'The truth,' said Henry, 'is that even now we don't begin to understand how "matter" (the brain) becomes "mind" (consciousness).' He looked at me across the table where we had been enjoying a late breakfast as festival guests. 'When we talk together now, it's all to do with the electro-chemical activity of our nerve cells, and yet our scientific world cannot begin to elucidate that.' It's an intriguing point: as individuals, we have a very limited experience of our mind's actual working. What, I wondered, about the twentieth century's advances in neuroscience? Will we ever break the old cerebral constraint that we can never really know what we know?

'I'm not going to predict the future of neuroscience,' he replied, 'but there are very many sound reasons to doubt whether we can ever make much progress. We cannot experiment on our own consciousness, and we certainly can't experiment on other people's. So the investigation must remain acutely *subjective*, and that's its fundamental limitation. Besides, medical science is probably at odds with our ethical concerns. What interests us most about ourselves is what makes us human, not what makes us neurologically complex. You can do some often rather nasty experiments on chimpanzees, but what that tells us about the human brain is actually quite limited.'

Who better to address the frailty of the ageing brain

than a man who has spent his professional life examining it under surgical lights? A year after our first meeting in Wells, having just begun to write *Every Third Thought*, I went to visit Henry at home in Wimbledon. I was coming to terms with the three principal ways a brain can fail – cancerous tumour; stroke or stroke-related illness such as aneurysm; and diseases such as Alzheimer's – and I wanted to explore the meaning of these failures with Henry, the eminent brain surgeon, one-to-one.

☽

South Park Road, London SW19, is a typical suburban street, with speed bumps to deter boy racers. Towards Wimbledon Hill, there's a comfortable world of bankers, architects, and surgeons. In the other direction, approaching Collier's Wood, it's appropriate that Marsh, who cherishes his lone-wolf identity, should live towards the more marginal end.

Henry's house, shaded by trees, presents a dark, cluttered exterior with boxes of discarded papers outside the front door. Inside, it's like stepping aboard a late-Victorian yawl, skippered by a veteran sea dog, a character from *Treasure Island*, perhaps. Captain Marsh is a passionate amateur woodworker who has designed every detail of the interior himself from the overflowing library to the study-cum-screening room upstairs to his own loft conversion, an attic eyrie reached by a treacherous wooden stairway that would not seem out of place on an old tea-clipper or in a scene from *Chitty-Chitty Bang-Bang*.

Up there, facing into the wind on Henry's crow's nest, and looking across Haydons Road Recreation Ground, the suburbs seem remote. You can smell the distant fields of merrie England, and see transatlantic jets circling to land at Heathrow. Glance down, and you discover a wild back garden, two sheds (one for woodworking; the other for guests), some sinister undergrowth, and three beehives, another of his private passions. Henry's domain perfectly mirrors his personality: highly idiosyncratic, full of delightful surprises, and offering unexpected vistas of opinion and imagination.

In the distance, on ragged green playing fields, I can see schoolboys in the mist kicking a muddy ball. I turn away, as I always do: I often find free movement – jogging, skipping, walking, or running – almost unbearable to watch, and still cannot bear to be reminded of my 'deficits'. At least these kids are far away.

Henry, who loves to exercise, is still fully active. As we discuss the mystery of the brain, he describes a daily regime which kicks off, first thing, with an energetic run, a cup of black coffee, freshly ground, and a cold shower. 'Cold water is good for "vagal tone",' he remarks, cheerfully instructing me in the mysterious activity of the vagus nerve, the extraordinarily long nerve that runs from the brain to the heart.

Henry has the air of a man driven by a need to challenge himself, who combines restless self-starting with infusions of high anxiety. His inner demons, however, seem to be fundamentally benign. *Do No Harm* reports his frequent explosive irritation, rage, and frustration, but, on our various meetings, I'm always surprised to find him projecting such an air of bonhomous serenity that ill temper and frustration seem strangers to his personality. Perhaps that's to do with the larger satisfaction of doing the thing he loves: brain surgery.

Marsh, now sixty-seven, has worked as a surgeon for about forty years. Both his parents are dead, his father at ninety-six from Alzheimer's, his mother from cancer. In *Do No Harm* he writes, in moving terms, of his mother drifting in and out of consciousness, sometimes lapsing into German, her first language. 'It's been a wonderful life,' she told her son on her deathbed. 'We have said everything there is to say.' Henry has a profound investment in 'a good death'. The better I came to know him, though, the more this robust veteran from the battlefields of neurosurgery admitted to being 'haunted by fears of senile dementia'.

When I ask exactly what that meant to him, Marsh recalls 'the grotesque caricatures of human beings I nursed when I worked as a psycho-geriatric nursing assistant in 1976, and also the hollow, though benign and decent shell, my admirable father became. It means being only interested in eating, and otherwise being lost, dribbling prostatically with trousers smelling of urine.'

As well as being thoughtful, humane, and articulate, Mr Marsh (as he's known to colleagues at St George's Hospital) is an ideal person with whom to explore the darker dimensions of cerebral failure. He has not only operated on hundreds of human brains, and studied thousands of brain scans, he has also reflected deeply on the meaning of his remarkable experience as a neurosurgeon, on the limits of human reason, and on his own errors of judgement.

'We often don't cure people with our interventions,' he admits, addressing a crux of modern medicine, 'we simply prolong their lives at a cost.' Marsh's firmly held belief is that, in neurosurgery, death is often a good outcome, compared to being left horribly disabled or in a persistent vegetative state. He recalls the times he has been woken in the night to adjudicate the appropriate response to a cerebral emergency. 'It's always easier to treat a patient than not to treat,' he tells me. 'But you're almost certainly going to create a disabled person at the cost of saving a life.' Marsh seems to despair at the impossibility of the task, and begins to speak about the disjunction between the act of surgery and the workings of the brain. 'Surgery,' he says, 'is still relatively crude compared to the delicacy of the cortex. At what point do you stop? At what age? For instance, if the patient is going to be left without language, is it worth it?

'And then,' Henry goes on, getting agitated, 'the question becomes: how bad is the disability? How many "good" results justify how many "bad" ones? That is very, very difficult to assess. If you decide you must treat everyone, you will generate a lot of human suffering, especially among families.'

Marsh digresses into anecdote, in the chatty way he prefers. 'The mother of a very good friend of mine had surgery for narrowing of the carotid arteries in her neck in her late seventies, to prevent a stroke. The operation was successful but she went on to develop Alzheimer's and became foul-mouthed and paranoid – completely out of keeping with her previous personality – and eventually died twelve years later in institutional care, doubly incontinent, etc.' The tone of his recollection darkens as he continues: 'It became difficult for her family to remember her as she was when well, as opposed to what she was when her brain was rotting and rotten.' Marsh seems troubled by the memory. 'Really, it would have been better if she had not had her carotid arteries operated upon, and had died from a stroke – or so it seems in retrospect.'

☾

Henry begins to explain his motives in writing *Do No Harm*. He is troubled by the casual tyranny exercised by his profession. 'As I approach the end of my career,' he says, 'I feel an increasing obligation to bear witness to past mistakes I have made, in the hope that my trainees will learn how not to make the same mistakes themselves.' He has a lecture, entitled 'All My Worst Mistakes', that's often heard in stunned silence by his audiences, where he likes to quote René Leriche in *La philosophie de la chirurgie* (1951): 'Every surgeon carries within himself a small cemetery, where from time to time he goes to pray – a place of bitterness and regret, where he must look for an explanation for his failures.'

Failure haunts brain surgery more than any other profession, and there's something quite compulsive about Marsh's confession. 'It's the professional shame that hurts the most,' he concedes with a rueful grin, his trademark. 'It's vanity really. As a neurosurgeon you have to come to terms with ruining people's lives and with making mistakes. But one still feels terrible about it. As a surgeon you float on the thermals of your patients' trust. However,' he continues, with cheerful pragmatism, 'you must learn to be objective about what you see, and yet not lose your humanity in the process.' Marsh admits that as a young doctor, he became 'hardened in the way that doctors have to become hardened', and also confesses that now he's reaching the end of his career, 'I am less frightened by failure, and can dare to be a little less detached.' Here, he begins to address his anxieties. 'Besides, with advancing age I can no longer deny that I am made of the same flesh and blood as my patients, and that I am equally vulnerable.'

Today, in the comfort of his home, I direct our conversation towards that most obvious vulnerability, his own fears about old age. 'I hope for a quick end,' he says, 'with a heart attack or stroke, preferably while asleep. But I realize that I may not be so fortunate.' What might that mean, from his experience? 'I may very well have to go through a time when I am still alive but have no future to hope for and only a past to look back on.' In that diminished condition, old age might seem like a new kind of mental torture, inexorably conditioned by cerebral atrophy. Marsh knows what dying can mean, and will pray for 'a good death'. How often does he think about this? 'About every third minute.' Another sheepish grimace. 'More often than sex.'

Like Andrew Lees, Henry believes that an exercise regime is the way to keep the brain healthy. 'The brain is a living organism,' he instructs. 'It's good to keep it busy and active, and stimulated by physical activity.'

'Mind and body,' he concludes, alluding to the classical wisdom of *mens sana in corpore sano*, 'are inseparable.'

Beyond these relatively simple areas of concern, there is the larger question of human consciousness, the *terra incognita* of neuroscience. Occasionally, for effect, he will say that we know less about the brain than we do about the infinite spaces of the universe. 'Nobody,' adds Henry, reverting to his favourite theme, 'can begin to explain consciousness. It seems to me highly unlikely that we'll ever work out how it operates.' This does not trouble him. 'As I get older,' he confides, 'I derive a certain spiritual consolation from this profound mystery, the origin of consciousness. You know' – his smile is almost mischievous – 'I find that quite appealing.'

It's here, inexorably, that the reflections of the brain surgeon begin to coincide with the inner life of the patient. This is a subject, with almost as much complexity as medicine itself, that precisely mirrors the fears and worries expressed by Henry Marsh. One classic statement of the patient's predicament can be found in *Devotions upon Emergent Occasions*, Meditation 5, where John Donne writes:

> As *Sickness* is the greatest misery, so the greatest misery of sicknes, is solitude . . . *Solitude* is a torment which is not threatened in *hell* itselfe.

In the course of growing old, there's one thing as certain as death (or taxes): at some point in the future we shall join an invisible grey army of reluctant conscripts. In doctors' waiting rooms, in hospitals, and in ambulances, we shall become 'the patient'.

9

ASTRIDE OF A GRAVE

'I feel monotony and death to be almost the same'

Charlotte Brontë, *Shirley*

As a long-term convalescent, with a history of steady neurological recovery, I have intimate experience of being a patient. During 2015/16, my own tally of tedious waiting, always with a book, but just as often with frustration, included three appointments for MRI scans at Queen Square; two waiting-room sessions to see my stroke consultant, Richard Greenwood; another in the National Hospital to see one of his colleagues, a professor of neurology; four appointments to see a hand-surgeon for an operation on Dupuytren's contracture; and another appointment for a DAT scan and more blood tests. Adding up this year's dead time, I calculate I spent the best part of two days in the waiting rooms of the medical profession. Such delays seem interminable; and you acquire new strategies. I have now mastered the art of appropriating other people's appointments. I am, no doubt, a bad patient.

In the popular mind, to be 'a patient' has connotations of submission, passivity, and acceptance. One serving nurse has addressed the contemporary association of the term: 'I am interested in this word because I think that nowadays the quality of being "patient" is essential to all staff who work on the frontline in the NHS. We all have to be "able to accept or tolerate delays, problems or suffering without becoming annoyed or anxious". This leaves me wondering: who is the patient?' Certainly, the invalid's experience of enforced isolation evokes a variety of responses.

As a sick person, you might find yourself to be more restless, angry, and difficult – 'im-patient' – than you expect. Here, etymology provides a helpful corrective. *Patient*, the noun, has nothing to do with tolerance; rather, it is all about suffering. The word itself originates in the Middle English *pacient*, from Anglo-French, and from Latin *patiens*, or the present participle of *patior* to suffer. The word's first known use comes in the fourteenth century when it refers to 'a sufferer, one who suffers patiently'. In 1484, the printer/publisher William Caxton connects the word to illness with 'Whan the pacyent or seke [sick] man sawe her . . .'

The experience of 'the patient' reinforces his or her solitude. Only patients can possibly understand what they are suffering. Hospitals are lonely places, especially at night. That isolation sponsors fear and uncertainty. The existential mystery of being unwell, towards the end of life, might become a consolation. It might also inspire the black realism of Samuel Beckett, in the words of Pozzo towards the end of *Waiting for Godot*:

One day he went dumb, one day I went blind, one day we'll go deaf, one day we were born, one day we shall die, the same day, the same second, is that not enough for you? They give birth astride of a grave, the light gleams an instant, then it's night once more.

Is this not a subtle allusion to that Anglo-Saxon sparrow fluttering through the smoky mead hall? Beckett's vision of man's fate is universal to the older self and that increasingly urgent internal dialogue about becoming reconciled to human 'insignificance' and getting lost in the infinity of time and space.

☽

In the realm of patient-hood, there can be few stranger tales than the twentieth-century experience of the survivors of the 'sleeping sickness' pandemic of 1916–17, a story reported in Oliver Sacks' medical classic, *Awakenings*, a book that has inspired short stories, poems, novels, and plays, notably Harold Pinter's *A Kind of Alaska*. Its central themes – falling asleep, being turned to stone, being awakened, decades later, to a world no longer one's own – grip the imagination like the best drama.

The 'sleeping sickness' pandemic of 1916–17, a development of Parkinsonism, ravaged the lives of nearly five million people before it disappeared, as suddenly and inexplicably as it had appeared, in 1927. A third of those afflicted by encephalitis lethargica, a virus of the mind that causes a kaleidoscope of bizarre neurological symptoms, died in its acute stages, usually in advanced states of coma. Patients who suffered an extremely severe somnolent/insomniac attack often failed ever to recover their original vitality, and lived out their days, cut off from humanity, in a deeply strange, inaccessible, frozen state ('a kind of Alaska'), oblivious to the passage of time, or what had befallen them.

'Patient' hardly begins to do justice to the torments endured by these survivors. Perhaps their best consolation was that they were unaware of their suffering, like 'extinct volcanoes' according to the doctor who first identified encephalitis lethargica. They would sit motionless and speechless all day in their chairs, totally lacking energy, impetus, initiative, motive, appetite, affect, or desire. According to Andrew Lees, who worked on British 'sleeping sickness' patients at Highlands Hospital in North London, it's a measure of the brain's inscrutability that the exact cause of this strange affliction is still a mystery. Everything about 'sleeping sickness' was capricious, he remembers. 'Nothing was predictable.' It was his job to 'decipher a chaos that appeared to defy the laws of pharmacology.'

In the majority of cases, these patients had their thoughts and feelings unchangingly fixed at the point at which their long 'sleep' had closed in on them. For many survivors, this was the 1920s, a time more real to them than any subsequent decade. Their minds remained clear and unclouded; and yet, unable to work or to see to their needs, frequently abandoned by their friends and families, these patients were put away in chronic hospitals, nursing homes, and lunatic asylums and forgotten, like lepers of the twentieth century. Yet some lived on, getting older and frailer, inmates of institutions, in Sacks' words 'profoundly isolated, deprived of experience, half-forgetting, half-dreaming of the world they once lived in.'

In 1969, after more than forty years of lives as insubstantial as ghosts and as passive as zombies, these 'extinct volcanoes', scattered in hospitals for chronic neurological disability in Britain, France and the USA, erupted into life through the intervention of a remarkable new drug, L-DOPA (laevodihydroxyphenylalanine), which had extraordinary 'awakening' powers. In one hospital in particular – the Beth Abraham in the Bronx, New York City – some eighty patients, long regarded as effectively moribund, returned explosively to life. Oliver Sacks was the brilliant young neurologist who administered the wonder drug. *Awakenings* became his account of a unique experience, the return to humanity of men and women whose personalities had become immured in post-encephalitic torpor.

Sacks kept meticulous notes on his patients' recovery. 'I cannot think back on this time without profound emotion', he wrote later. 'It was the most significant and extraordinary moment in my life, no less than in the lives of our patients. All of us at Mount Carmel [Beth Abraham] were caught up with the emotion, the excitement, with something akin to enchantment, even awe.'

Sacks' stories become a kind of memoir, a neurological romance and a profoundly sympathetic essay on the human condition. For me, at this point in my journey, *Awakenings* teaches many lessons. In hospital, as patients, suffering the torments of isolation, two things occur, in opposition: we lose our individuality, joining the continuum of the unwell, while becoming more self-obsessed, having the leisure for introspection. Here, in the hospital bed, we can reflect on God's conundrum: *he gives us life, and an irrepressible instinct for it, but not a clue about death, or how and when we will die.* I know from experience that, as patients, we experience the flow of Time as acutely as any lover. The hours, minutes, and seconds make up days that form into a pattern of interminable waiting – for visitors, nurses, doctors, and surgeons – punctuated by irruptions of treatment. But set those moments against the historical panorama of humanity, and they seem trifling. This, too, becomes another dimension of 'insignificance'.

For the patient, this plays out as another version of the mind–body problem. Patients suffer physical afflictions, of course, but the real battle is fought inside their head: matters of life and death become, fundamentally, matters of consciousness, and the stories that patients tell themselves. In our own time, the post-war generation has too much of an investment in willpower to welcome a new narrative over which they have no control.

And here's the rub. The real world is both achingly precious and, at the same time, indifferent to our plight. The sun goes down, the tides ebb and flow, and the rain rains every day, steady and relentless, as it has always done. Elsewhere, the landscape shifts a bit here and there but – this side of the next Ice Age – essentially, it remains immutable, resilient, and settled. Even with global warming, the planet's continuities seem to dominate the discontinuities. Let's be optimistic. Resilience is possibly one of Earth's best qualities, and one that continues to shape the lives of its inhabitants.

The patient becomes a microcosm of humanity. Considering our response to illness and mortality, it seems to me that humanity tells stories, or makes new tunes, to be at peace with its eternal predicaments. During the course of 2015/16, I arrived at the conviction that the internal dialogue provoked by 'every third thought' can only be resolved through narrative. Once upon a time, that was the role of religion. But what kind of self-justifying stories can patients tell themselves to sustain their resilience in an age without faith? The short answer – following the theme of this book – has been the assertion of the self, in that cocktail of optimism and defiance we call willpower.

It is perhaps part of humanity's intrinsic nobility of spirit that very many individuals, facing the inevitable endgame, discover an urge to be positive and undaunted. For the anonymous patient, grappling with 'insignificance', this becomes a reassertion of identity and meaning. Willpower often tells another story. And so, often amid degradation, sorrow, and despair, there are many inspiring tales of grace, courage, and dignity.

10

THE WILL TO LIVE

'People's capacity to survive, one way or another, loss and even devastation is at once a banal and remarkable fact. The sheer stubbornness of the so-called "will to live" is often cause for celebration.'

Adam Phillips, *Darwin's Worms*

For my friend Kate, a woman just in her fifties, but who could easily pass for a seasoned forty-something, the battle between ill-health and self-esteem has been fought in mind and body, at the front line of sickness, and in close combat.

At times, it can feel as if breast cancer among the middle-aged women of the twenty-first century has become an epidemic. Fifteen years ago, when my sister Elizabeth survived a brutal encounter with the disease, bravely facing down its threats, I learned at first hand its traumatic effects on family life. In March 2016, I was completing a first draft of this book when Kate, an experienced broadcaster, emailed with the news that she had recently been diagnosed with an aggressive Grade 3 tumour in her left breast.

In the UK, some sixty thousand women will be diagnosed with breast cancer every year: that's one every ten minutes. As everyone knows, breast cancer remains inexorably a killer, but 85 per cent of patients will survive beyond five years, a figure that a woman in Kate's position must cling to. Her awareness of life's transience has paradoxically strengthened her life, renewing her natural kindness, good humour, sympathy, and candour. All of this, remarkably, has flowed from the exercise of her willpower.

Kate has always been blessed with an irrepressible joie de vivre. Her determination to grapple with the shadows of ill-health as part of the human condition has made her, strangely, more alive than ever. Kate is singular and exceptional, but she is not unique. Defiance is essential to 'the will to live', but so is optimism. She has never been less than courageous, positive, and optimistic.

'I think I've been lucky,' she begins when, a few days later, we talk it over together in a cafe one spring afternoon in Notting Hill. Outside, the world is drenched in April sunshine, and bursting with new growth. Within, not even Kate's defiance can quite dispel the menace of cancer's deathly fingers. 'I do now wonder about my luck,' she repeats, turning over the latest sequence of events in her life. Not only had her tumour been caught early, her diagnosis was the fortunate outcome of a bureaucratic cock-up.

All women over fifty in Britain are entitled to an NHS scan every three years: Kate had been given the all-clear just a year before. But then, inexplicably, she was called in by her local hospital for another routine mammogram. In the midst of a busy life, she decided to go. When she arrived for this appointment, the receptionist seemed confused by the mistake, but said, 'You're here now, so if you want to have it . . .'

Kate replied, 'How many women are in front of me?'

'Just two.'

'So I thought,' she continues, 'all right then, I'll have it. But now – had I been told, There are six women waiting in front of you – I wonder if I might not have said, "Oh, stuff it," and gone home.' She laughs. 'So I consider myself to have been lucky.' We reflect on the strange tricks of chance. She admits that her fear of dying was trumped by the more immediate fear of mutilation.

'In the two-week period between being called back for more tests and the final diagnosis of cancer, obviously I was frightened of dying, but I was also really, really, frightened of losing my breasts. Here I am – I thought – I'm a fifty-four-year-old woman. I've already had to go through the indignities of the menopause. Evolution has already told me that I'm useless. Now I'm going to lose my breasts – and my hair – which I've always thought were a rather good feature.'

In fact, Kate found her luck holding: 'One of my first questions to the surgeon was, "What am I going to lose?"' When he replied that he thought he would be able to perform a lumpectomy, and save her left breast, Kate says, 'I felt this incredible sense of relief.'

Her oncologist embarked on treatment with bewildering speed. Even with her 'luck', Kate could not escape an overwhelming sense of a malignant Fate. 'I don't believe in God,' she remarks, 'but I did come to imagine a wrathful Greek god who was taking revenge on womankind. I mean, can you think of a more evil disease than one where they strip away your breasts, and make you lose your hair? Isn't that a kind of torture?'

When she met with her surgeon after the initial diagnosis, Kate's profound relief that she did not require a mastectomy still came with some unwelcome news. Her treatment would involve six weeks of radiotherapy, and 'probably' (in their consulting rooms, doctors cultivate euphemistic imprecision) some chemo as well. She was alarmed at the prospect of intensive radiotherapy. The more she looked at it, the bigger the commitment of time – five days a week for six weeks – which seemed to threaten her professional life. But then: more luck.

Kate heard from a close friend about a radical new treatment known as IORT (inter-operative radiotherapy). This involves cutting out the growth, then targeting the tumour bed and 'zapping the cancer'. Kate immediately put on her journalistic hat and contacted the surgeon involved, who proudly told her how successful his trials had been.

Kate began to press for the new treatment at once. For her, the attractions were obvious: IORT would mean a one-off session of radiotherapy. (Kate's tumour was over her heart, and her consultant had advised her that there was still some doubt about 'the long term effects of radiotherapy on the heart'.) IORT would minimize the irradiation of the cancer so close to a vital organ.

Kate's IORT would be performed on the day of her lumpectomy. 'Zapping the cancer at once seemed a good idea,' says Kate, in her breezy and forceful way. 'I was going to take control of this. That's the kind of person I am.' Accordingly, at the appointed time, her surgeon performed the operation, and then the German-designed IORT machine was wheeled into position. Kate's wound, and the tumour bed, was 'zapped' for forty minutes with a single, targeted beam. There was no burning to the skin (a typical side-effect of conventional radiotherapy), and afterwards the surgeons sewed her up. 'I went home the same day,' says Kate, quietly triumphant. 'I was back at work a week later.'

Still, she had undergone a life-changing trauma. Today, on this sunny spring afternoon, with her surgery behind her, but still in the midst of chemotherapy, Kate speaks, candidly and with some passion, about her fears in retrospect. As well as her fate as a woman, there was also her sudden and poignant fragility as a human being. She found herself lying awake at night, 'feeling really, really frightened', and sobbing uncontrollably in the dark. 'I was imagining the worst,' she continues. 'What if the cancer had spread? What if it was all over me? What if . . . ?' Kate stops: those had been unthinkable thoughts.

In the complex transaction between mind and body, I have often speculated about whether it is possible to influence, or even cure, an illness by taking thought. People talk about 'fighting' cancer with 'a positive mental attitude'. During my convalescence in the years after my stroke, I would sometimes affect a 'no surrender' attitude which at least made me feel better about my unresolved and chronic disabilities. Some stroke-recoverers even punish their bodies in the hope of firing up pathways of neuro-plasticity.

In my experience, thoughts more often tip the other way into the abyss of 'What if?'. What if I never walk freely again? What if, with ageing, my mobility becomes seriously restricted? What if I fall in a crowded street? What if my instability is connected to neuro-degeneration? What if I can no longer function in the working world? These 'What ifs?' seem to offer the prospect of isolation, solitude, and prolonged physical restriction. Cabin'd, cribb'd, confin'd, like Macbeth, we become prey to saucy doubts and fears. All this, of course, takes place in our hyper-active and hyper-imaginative brains. For the successful breast-cancer patient, the catalogue of 'What ifs?' is almost infinite.

Later in our conversation, reflecting on these desolate moments, but speaking carefully, as if feeling her way into a difficult subject, Kate admits: 'I wish I did believe in something. I've certainly felt that . . . the need . . . In those days when I was waiting to hear if I'd got it or not – and I was convinced that I did – in those moments, when you're so frightened it's as though the blood running through your veins is ice-cold, then I did wish I believed in God.'

Kate says her need was simple: 'Belief would have given me someone to ask for help.' Instead, she turned to friends and family, people to whom she could voice her fears. 'I quickly came to understand that breast cancer is not the killer it used to be,' she says. 'I would tell myself: "You can survive this. You'll be all right."' She smiles with some of her old confidence. 'So I suppose that became my belief.' Joking, she refers to another friend who has been living with cancer for a while. 'She says: "I can live with the sword of Damocles hanging over me, but I don't want to have to polish the fucking thing." I think that sums up my attitude perfectly. You do get ever so slightly tired of being told to get on with your life.'

Questions about the future, near or far, remain part of the battle with ill-health. Kate is having to make that adjustment, but her natural optimism will help. From my experience, after twenty years, I still feel excitement at the thrill of the unknown, at least until those pesky 'What ifs?' show up. But those creatures do not have to be malign. Maybe they will show the way to new worlds and possibilities? Survive a brain attack and you acquire a special kind of resilience. I like to think I am equal to whatever the future holds, prepared for what fate holds in store. In the predicament of grappling with the 'What ifs?', all one can do is keep a sharp eye out for opportunity, and sail forward under the flag of 'No surrender'.

Kate, who describes herself as 'a naturally positive person', has also found consolation in literature and the arts. Later in her convalescence, she described going to the Edinburgh Festival, and happily sitting through five new plays a day: 'If I'm reading a good book, or watching a play, or listening to a beautiful piece of music, I'm transported elsewhere, and can forget about my cancer. I've become an addict of very good podcasts, and I've joined Audible.com.' She adds, merrily, and with some astonishment, that she's been 'listening to a lot of Trollope'. Barchester aside, Kate has some advice for fellow sufferers. 'I'd suggest doing things that give you pleasure rather than trawling cancer-survivor websites. I went onto one of those websites last night, and ended up wanting to throw my laptop away, and return to my novel.'

In the absence of faith, I asked her, 'What might dying mean?' Kate's answer, which speaks to her determination to live in the present moment, came as a surprise. 'My greatest fear,' she replies, 'was about those I would be leaving behind.' Kate describes how her husband had already lost a child from his previous marriage. 'I know what grief looks like,' she says sadly. 'My main thought was: I can't do this to my husband and my son. I just can't die on them. What would they do?' Her concerns seemed to be less about her mortality, and more about the vitality of her marriage and her family.

'I'm a mother and a lover,' she continues. 'I have a very good marriage. I worried about the sexual relationship I would have with my husband if I lost my breast. All of these things went through my mind, including: would I be less attractive? It all sounds very superficial next to Death, but it really isn't – it was all about my identity as a woman.'

At this point in our conversation, Kate became almost indignant. 'Am I dying as a woman? I might get to live, but will I be only half a woman? Half of myself?' And of course, she could not prevent the apprehension of Death from shining a bright, unbearable light on her past life. Everyone carries inside them the memories of youth. 'I smoked, I drank, and I partied,' says Kate. 'I've always lived life to the full.' It's another irony of this story that those who make the most of their lives sometimes seem to pay a higher price. In extremis, the carefree past can become a terrible reproach.

Kate's surgeon had counselled her not to dwell too much on the 'why?' of her illness. Still, she freely confesses that her cancer had been 'a wake-up call'. She insists now that once her chemotherapy is complete, she will respond to this emergency. With another cheerful, ironical laugh, she adds that she now has a new aspiration – the 'ambition to change' her way of life.

Kate's chemotherapy treatment has been a huge strain, on her and on her family. To mitigate the side-effects, she consumes a supermarket bag full of drugs: 'anti-aching pills, anti-rash pills, anti-vomiting pills, sleeping pills . . .' Finally, however, she seems to be coming through. With the sessions drawing to a close, but much weakened, she tires easily, lacks the energy for exercise, and cannot rest at night. 'My body feels really tired, but I still can't sleep. That's awful. My mind is racing, and I've not slept through the night since I was diagnosed. At first it was stress, now it's the side-effects of the drugs.'

Still, Kate has begun to approach a new serenity, as if purged by the experience of coming face to face with her mortality: 'I'm not that frightened any more. I feel secure in the advances that have been made in breast-cancer treatment in the last ten years. Only a few years ago, I would have had a full mastectomy. Things have changed. Chemotherapy has become less punishing. When my chemo is complete, I will have a 95 per cent chance of being well in five years' time. I'd say that's pretty good.'

We both digest this statistic in silence. Then Kate says, 'I have these moments when I ask myself, "What if the NHS hadn't called me back? What if I'd walked away from that mammogram?" It feels like a close shave.' A small, but grateful smile of victory. 'I feel like I got away with it.'

11

THE PERSON WHO WAS ILL

'I have wrestled with death. It is the most unexciting contest you can imagine. It takes place in an impalpable greyness, with nothing underfoot, with nothing around, without spectators, without clamour, without glory, without the great desire of victory, without the great fear of defeat, in a sickly atmosphere of tepid scepticism, without much belief in your own right, and still less in that of your adversary.'

Joseph Conrad, *Heart of Darkness*

Kate's courage is all the more impressive for being expressed in the shadow of extinction. She has had to face up to, and be terrified by, the prospect of dying. And yet, for some baby-boomers, such a rendezvous with reality is unthinkable. For them, the self is king and the body sovereign, while they must be immortal. On the spectrum of reactions to the human predicament, this might seem an extreme response, but it does demonstrate an unquenchable will to live, the quality that makes us human.

Carol is fifty-one, a successful policy consultant,

married with two grown-up children whose childhood was shaped by their mother's serious illness. This is Carol's story, and it's one I've been vaguely conscious of, as her friend, for several years. She has never spoken about her chronic afflictions before, and her words flow in eloquent sentences, as if too long pent up. This is less of a conversation, and more of a monologue, into which I feel lucky occasionally to insert an observation, or perhaps even an enquiry. Carol, no question, likes to command her own narrative.

'My first bout of ill health,' she says, 'began about twenty years ago, with an episode of food poisoning that never seemed to stop. I ignored it for a long time: I was brought up in a household where you didn't make a fuss about things. Besides, I'd always been phenomenally – even rudely – healthy. My family had lived in Kenya and Botswana, where everyone got sick all the time. That was just part of everyday life, and you learned to get on with it.' Carol was firmly committed to the idea that she had an iron constitution, but on this occasion her body let her down. She remembers saying to her husband, 'I feel so ill I'm going to have difficulty walking up the stairs,' but then thinking, 'What utter nonsense. Stop exaggerating.'

In her kitchen, where we are sitting, Carol pauses to serve mint tea, then picks up where she left off. 'Eventually, I went to work but was physically too weak to move.' When, finally, she capitulated and went to see a consultant, he advised her that she was on the verge of 'a total collapse', suffering from colitis, a vicious auto-immune digestive disease. It would be five months before she was well enough to get out of bed and return to work. Looking back, she says, quite matter-of-fact, that, 'This disease has blighted my whole life. My son asked me the other day, "Why didn't you take us to museums at the weekend?" I replied that this had been the plan for his childhood, but I got ill when he was four.'

The whole experience left her baffled and amazed. She had always thought she was a fundamentally healthy person who was inexplicably unwell, and that her body would recover. 'I had been brought up with a mind-set that says, "Willpower can do anything,"' she remarks. 'My mother is very impatient of illness, from a stiff-upper-lip, get-on-with-it school of ill-health. I remember her telling me that "Max Weber says illness is social deviance – and I agree with Max Weber."'

Carol certainly felt she was a social deviant, as far as her own chronic condition was concerned, and decided 'the less said about it the better'. When she was unwell, she would stay at home and sleep. 'I didn't want people to think of me as feeble. I thought, "This is hideously embarrassing." I don't want to think about it, and it's bound to stop soon.'

But it didn't. Soon, she was back with the consultant, who told her she was getting so weak that, as he put it, 'You will die.' The upshot of this stark warning was that Carol took early retirement for medical reasons, which came as 'a deep relief', and yet it never occurred to her that she was fatally ill. Indeed, when advised that she risked dying, her first thought was, '"How interesting."

I was delighted by how dramatic I'd become. Plus, I simply did not believe my consultant.'

The decision to stop work was much more threatening to her than any fear of dying. She confesses she was scared of losing her identity. The months in which she was too ill to go to her desk were, she says, 'terrifying'. Carol is a highly intelligent, thoughtful and decisive woman, and this account of herself comes as a shock. I wondered if, in extremis, she had ever thought about discussing her illness with friends.

'No, I never wanted to talk about it, or draw anyone's attention to the fact that I was unwell. I just didn't want to be "The Person Who Was Ill". Actually, my children were worried more than me. My daughter was about six when she asked me if I was going to die.' To which Carol replied, briskly: 'Of course not.' Her coping mechanisms are as iron-clad as Kate's sense of humour, but I find it hard to believe that she never had moments of introspection, and now challenged her obdurate denial.

Carol, however, will not be shaken. 'No, my reaction was always: "What is this thing that is being imposed upon me? Could someone please take it away? How unreasonable it is that I should have to suffer this inconvenience." No, it caused me no introspection whatever for many years. None.' She flashes an ironic but steely smile, like a scalpel. 'Just fury.'

Carol is the kind of woman you want in a crisis: sometimes, she can seem quite astonishingly calm and collected. But now she was on the brink of losing her cool. She goes on: 'I was infuriated and bewildered. I felt guilty and ashamed for not functioning better. I did think, at some level, that I must have done this to myself, and that there was something I was doing that was wrong. At the same time, I felt like Thomas the Tank Engine. I just had to keep going.'

I manage to insert a question in the conversation: 'Did you ever explore any kind of therapy?'

'No.' A beat. At one point, she added, her consultant had asked her to see a psychiatrist 'just in case I was depressed', and to discover if depression was a source of the illness. To this, Carol's sarcastic response was, 'Yes, I am sometimes depressed – but that's because of my illness, not vice versa.'

Eventually, she did go and see a psychoanalyst. This, she adds, almost merrily, was 'the single worst experience of my whole life. I felt as if I had been assaulted, and then discarded.' As we review this phase of her profound ill-health, our conversation seems to have reached a natural pause, and then she says, quite bluntly. 'Six years ago, I was diagnosed with breast cancer.'

☽

Carol's experience of this diagnosis repeated the experience of her first illness: she was wholly unprepared. 'I'd had my children early, had breast-fed them and so on. I always ate well, with plenty of fruit and vegetables. I didn't smoke or drink much. I went running. I'm not the kind of person who gets cancer, I thought. I was so sure of my fitness that when I went for a second appointment, I didn't even take my husband.'

As it turned out, Carol's cancer was fast-growing

and aggressive. But now a new crisis presented itself. She had to have an immediate operation and, at the same time, come off all her colitis drugs. She'd been on immune-suppressants for more than five years. Her cancer doctor wanted to stop this treatment. All at once her body became a battleground between her cancer specialist and the doctors who were treating her chronic digestive problems. In the end, to tackle the cancer, she underwent two operations, followed by eight sessions of chemotherapy.

Carol's cancer treatment, she reports with characteristic stoicism, was 'pretty grim'. For the first time in all her years of ill-health, Carol says she was frightened on two levels. 'First, there was this horrible sense of being caught between two medical protocols, the oncologists and the digestive specialists. Secondly, I was very, very surprised' – this must be the mother of understatements – 'by chemotherapy. It was like nothing I'd ever experienced. I'd once had a bad attack of malaria which had been so unendurable I would have been thrilled to be dead. Chemo was far worse than that. When you are ill, you can feel your body fighting something. That's what the fever is about, the battle to get better. With chemo, you can feel you are being poisoned, and that every cell in your body is wavering on the edge of death. My head ached. Everything – even water – tasted disgusting. I was too feeble to move. After each session, I would be curled up at home, scarcely alive, waiting for the next stage.'

The real terror of chemo was the thought that she was going mad with 'chemo brain'. She'd open the morning newspaper, and would not be able to follow the news. 'That was the most terrifying thing that's ever happened to me,' she confesses. 'All my life, I've been able to read and digest words very quickly. Now I could not follow A plus B plus C; i.e. if this, then that. I could read novels, but I simply could not follow an argument.'

Some patients develop detachment. This was not Carol's response. She has, she admits, 'a rather narrow sense of personal value'. Instead, she asserted herself, went to see her consultant, and told him, 'I'm stopping this, I'd rather die.' Commendably, her consultant advised her that she could not do this to her family, that her brain would recover, and that there was this nasty option (chemotherapy) – or death.

'Now,' says Carol, 'I was in a state of private panic. I didn't tell anyone, apart from the doctors and my husband.'

When she was first diagnosed, Carol found her personal crisis strangely exhilarating. 'I was fed up with the routine of my life. At least this was interesting.' Now, in the depths of chemo, she says she discovered a new source of solace: the extraordinary kindness of friends and strangers, and a tidal wave of love and affection. 'When people know that you are close to the edge, they will come and tell you extraordinary things. I think people feel very emotional and engaged around the seriously unwell.'

I interject to remind her of Keats' remark that 'We are all ill'.

'Yes,' replies Carol. 'Illness strips everything away. There are suddenly no barriers. In that situation, people want to say something real, to come up with a matching reality. And the most "real" things they can say are the secret things that they don't normally talk about. They believe – rightly – that you will honour their predicament.'

For Carol, everything in the world became quite extraordinarily vivid. 'I still didn't think I was going to die, but the experience did wake me up. Everything seemed so worthy of attention. It changed, and deepened my relationship with everyone around me.' She is not starry-eyed about this, as one might expect. 'I think everyone has some sympathy with a limited crisis. Almost everyone behaved well. There were some funny moments. I remember one colleague, with whom I'd had a slightly combative relationship, gave me a book as a present: *The Importance of the Breast in Western Culture*.'

☽

When she looks back on nearly twenty years of chronic ill-health, Carol has a few regrets: 'Being unwell teaches you to value things. I've had moments of great joy. I feel fortunate.'

Carol's passionate optimism encompasses her general attitude to matters of life and death. Speaking of her breast cancer, which is now well behind her, she believes that the treatment – a horrendous experience – was good for her. It made her more appreciative of everything, of being alive. It also released her from what she calls 'the unconscious voices of puritan guilt'. We both agree that driving yourself towards any intangible goal is at once a path to disaster, and also pointless. You have to recognize the value of what you've got. 'Thanks to the cancer,' she concludes, 'I've found so many more moments of joy and contentment.'

Carol also believes that acute and persistent ill-health has renewed her focus on the things that matter. 'I've grown intolerant,' she continues, 'of things that waste time. I've learned to interrogate my choices as a way of enjoying things more.'

As we reviewed her strange story, I wondered if she had ever felt the victim of a malign fate.

'God, no. When I was growing up in the Third World, I saw countless lives ripped apart by war, disease, famine, and poverty. For most people, life is awful, random, and savage. Me? I'm living one of the luckiest lives imaginable.'

Finally, I decide I must ask the woman who does not believe in death if she ever thinks about what dying might be like. Her answer is strangely predictable. 'I never do, no,' she replies. 'I just don't think about it at all.' But then she confesses to a deep fear of dementia, and a loss of cognitive competence, and reports that she has given her children power of attorney for her old age. Robust and unsentimental as ever, Carol says, 'Looking hopeless and vacant for twenty years in a nursing home is just not worth it.'

Here she slips into an affecting personal recollection. 'My dear father had dementia for the last eighteen months of his life. It was absolute torture for him – and for my poor mother. He had a variant which meant that a lot of his faculties were fine. He could discuss issues of global inequality, or the failings of American foreign policy. At the same time, he also believed that my mother had vanished, and that he was living with an impostor. This was something that caused him the deepest distress. He'd phone me to say, "I've lost the only woman I've ever really loved – can you please find her for me?" And my mother would be in the room next door. It was hell for both of them. Suddenly they were lost to each other. Occasionally, he would weep in desperation. He was not actually mad, but' – this part of our conversation seems suddenly difficult – 'I could never conceive of a situation in which I would kill him.'

Looking into the future, Carol continues, 'By the time I'm old, I hope a doctor would make that choice for me.' She becomes almost indignant. 'I think it's a travesty of what life is about that we should keep people alive through these vacant years. We know that old people are often not treated well. Carers get fed up with mad old people. As a society, we've got our priorities so topsy-turvy. Why pour all these resources into the miserable and pointless ends of people's lives? It makes no sense.'

It seems to me that such a well-educated family would surely have discussed the right to die. In his lucid moments, I wonder, did her father ever discuss euthanasia?

'He did ask me,' she replies, with a kind of sorrow, 'but I could not do it. I could see that it was the right thing to do, and I wish the system had allowed it.' Carol describes how, after a bad fall, her demented father's life had been prolonged by the well-meaning intervention of the local hospital, a source of further agony to her mother. 'He could have died within days,' she says, 'and everyone would have been happy.' With a certain finality, she adds, 'That's as much as I think about death. Even when I consider the statistics of breast cancer, and how they might apply to me, I principally think: "What a delicious, and dramatic, statement this could make."' While I marvel at her fearless and thrilling egocentricity, Carol goes on: 'What I think about dying is that I think I'm immortal, though of course I know I'm not.'

There remains her anxiety about suffering her father's fate, and Carol comments wryly that we seem to have reached a stage where longevity begins to seem worse than death. 'When my brain starts to fade,' says Carol, 'if I seem at all doolally, and my brain has gone, please get someone to kill me.'

This, finally, is the clincher: Carol has endured the torments of chemo, and has lived with the imminence of mortality for years, and remains resolutely unfazed by death, yet can be visibly disturbed by the prospect of neurological degeneration.

When we come to reflect on how we die, it's longevity combined with a neuro-degenerative disease – Parkinson's or Alzheimer's, for instance – that has become the dominant preoccupation of an ageing population. According to Andrew Lees, Parkinson's is 'the commonest neurological cause of chronic physical handicap in the elderly'. He concedes that its cause is not really known (intriguingly, it's twice as common among non-smokers). The disease will often begin with maladroitness in one hand, and feelings of tiredness. It's the emergence of a tremor that cannot be ignored and usually leads to a specialist referral.

That was how Max, a sixty-seven-year-old retired journalist, found himself in Andrew Lees's consulting rooms, and faced with the news of a condition that would, ultimately, kill him. By chance, this was a diagnosis I'd encountered several years before, with my own father's Parkinson's.

12

WHERE ARE WE GOING?

'No man amongst us [is] so sound, of so good a constitution, that hath not some impediment of body or mind.'

Robert Burton, *The Anatomy of Melancholy.*

When my father, Michael McCrum, died on 16 February 2005, aged eighty-one, his was an archetypal good exit. He passed away with incipient Parkinson's and a dormant cancer of the prostate, but it was a case of 'with' not 'from', an all-important distinction. Remarkably, indeed, when he had first told his family about the Parkinson's diagnosis, he had even predicted this outcome; and I don't think he ever intended to live into extreme old age in a state of progressive debilitation. At the moment he collapsed in the living room of the terraced house in Cambridge to which, after a distinguished academic career, he had retired with my mother, he was felled by catastrophic cardiac arrest, not the illness once known as 'palsy'. My father's condition as a Parkinson's sufferer was still in the early stages: his symptoms were under control, his magisterial presence as commanding as ever, and his brilliant mind fully alive, as it always had been. I think he was lucky. Wholly in character, he made a quick getaway, as he always preferred to do when alive. When I was recovering in hospital in 1995, he would sit at my bedside and read aloud from P. G. Wodehouse. I miss him still, and think of him every day.

These were the moments that came flooding back when I first went to meet Max – known to his friends as 'Mack' – at the end of 2015, taking memories of my father's final months.

And yet, I was surprised to find only the faintest echo of those afflictions. At his home in West London, overlooking Richmond Park, Max was a picture of serenity, and even well-being. It was only as I got to know him better that hints of his condition began to emerge. Rather typically, Max had given his illness a nickname – 'Parky's' – and had also been reading up on its history like the good reporter he is. This, I recognized later, was part of his coming to terms with the sombre truth of his affliction. Unlike Kate, or Carol, here was a man who had to make peace with the idea that there is no cure— a sensible strategy.

It was in 1817 that Dr James Parkinson, a London physician, published *On the Shaking Palsy*, the first essay to identify and describe the symptoms of what is now known as Parkinson's disease. Dr Parkinson's account of his patients' characteristic tremors and their distinctive hurrying of gait and speech was not exactly new. In *Brief Lives*, John Aubrey had already given a description of the 'shaking palsy' suffered by the great English philosopher Thomas Hobbes. An inveterate gossip, Aubrey was not breaking much new ground, either. As Oliver Sacks writes in *Awakenings*, such symptoms had been described by 'physicians back to the time of Galen'. Crucially, it was Dr Parkinson who 'first saw every feature and aspect of the illness as a whole, and who presented it as a distinctive human condition or *form of behaviour.*'

For Max, the diagnosis of Parkinson's identified a fundamentally conventional version of the illness. At this early stage, on our first meeting, his symptoms, which were barely detectable, were being treated by daily doses of Azilect and Sinemet. To anyone who did not know him, Max might have seemed elderly and deliberate in his movements, but otherwise unimpaired. I suspect that any of his friends who had not have seen him for a few months would have noticed a slowing-down of Max's vigorous younger self, but not much else.

Max was born in December 1945 to Australian parents, who had moved to Britain with the coming of peace. He is a lifelong metropolitan who enjoys a comfortable retirement not far from the Thames as it winds through waterlogged meadows towards Hampton Court. He has three grown-up daughters, and he now lives with Jacky, his American partner, a globe-trotting journalist who has made their London home a sanctuary of elegance and tranquillity. Max describes himself as a broadcaster, but during his long career in the media he has also been a journalist and screenwriter, film director and TV producer. Above all, he is renowned for his documentary reporting.

Max's family are Scots-Irish, as mine are, which

perhaps explains some of our affinity. When we talked together in his upstairs sitting room with its distant view of the river, I think we both valued sharing the experience of cerebral deficits, comparing stroke with palsy. In his company, I recognize a gritty determination not to give in which I cannot help but admire. During my own convalescence, after 1995, I had adopted a 'no surrender' approach to ill-health that Max, who is a stranger to self-pity, seems to share. The 'Mack' I have come to know is a warm, witty, and engaging family man, a sharp raconteur with a strong sense of the ridiculous combined with an instinctive delight in the human comedy, especially the works of P. G. Wodehouse.

Max's diagnosis of Parkinson's did not come out of a clear blue sky. His appointment with Andrew Lees simply confirmed, and finally acknowledged, his suppressed anxiety about some unexplained and niggling new symptoms. During one of our conversations, he described how he had always wanted to go skating at Somerset House at Christmas. It was years since he'd done any skating, so he had enrolled in a couple of lessons. That was when he first discovered his body betraying him. 'I found that it didn't matter how many times I went to practise,' he said. 'I would always have this shaky sort of unsteadiness.'

For Max, this 'unsteadiness' (typical of Parkinson's) was a new and troubling sensation. 'Fit?' he queries. 'I had always been completely fit. Blessed, really. At least until 2015. That was when everything went wrong. I realize now that I must have been getting Parkinson's the previous year.' The onset of this disease is slow. Characteristic symptoms of the 'shaking palsy', described by Sacks and others, were now becoming present in his life, but not yet distressing. Manifestations of Parkinsonism at this stage could be checked by drugs. Compared to the remorseless cruelty of Alzheimer's, as Lees had advised me during our conversation in his lab, 'there is always something you can do to help a Parkinson's patient.'

Max is neatly dressed in khakis and a white shirt, and looks perfectly well, until you notice how stiffly he is sitting on the sofa, and how awkward his movement when he rises. 'There were other, odd little symptoms,' he says, 'but I'd ignored them. I remember going for walks on holiday that year, and I would keep falling behind Jacky. Yet, in the past, I had been a speedy, vigorous walker, steaming ahead on the path, and having to wait for everyone else to catch up. And then I started to get where I couldn't remember a word, or would get held up on people's names. That's what comes back to each now, when I think about it.'

I suggest that it's a typical human response to hope for the best while privately preparing for the worse. Max nods. With hindsight, he concedes that he did not want to confront his anxieties, or the possibility of becoming disabled. He admits, 'I had always been a little bit impatient with disabled people. Very arrogant, but there it is.'

☽

At first, Max's response to the diagnosis of the long-term death sentence of Parkinson's was characteristically phlegmatic. 'No,' he continues, 'I wasn't particularly appalled. Maybe I was expecting it.' He'd already had several consultations with his GP, followed by a visit to a specialist, before his appointment with Professor Lees. Finally, when the news came, he says, 'it was no big surprise.' Except for this: such infirmity was new to him. 'I had always taken my health for granted.'

Like Carol and Kate, and in a manner typical of this generation, he met the challenge presented by Parkinson's with a good measure of natural confidence. 'I don't remember being panicked, perhaps because I'd been very well briefed by people early on. The local NHS Parkinson's nurse, for instance, has been quite brilliant. There's a wonderful support system in Richmond. Round here, they have regular monthly meetings, for Parkinson's sufferers, which I have to admit I don't go to. That's partly because I don't feel I belong there. Yet. Everyone seems so old and shaky and doddery. The medication I'm on is quite successful, though I've no idea how long that will last.' He adds, with what I come to recognize as characteristic determination, that his New Year's resolution is 'to read more, think more, and exercise more'. Now he's a man with a plan. 'I'm going to make my Parkinson's my number one job.'

Max is nothing if not a realist. When we talk about his response to ill-health, he is quite frank about the possible outcomes. Parkinson's is a neuro-degenerative disease he is likely to die from. He knows what this means, and confides en passant, as a kind of afterthought, that his father had also suffered from it. A discreet pause punctuates the conversation. 'Jacky knows, of course,' he says. 'But I haven't told my daughters yet.' Pressed, he does concede that he has been 'a bit of a coward about this'.

Our conversation falters again, and then he adds. 'This diagnosis has come ten years sooner than I would have liked.'

Max is practical and stoical. 'I don't think "Why me?" ' he remarks, of his fate. 'I mean, "Why not me?" These things happen to millions of people. Why I should be immune to common experience? So, it's a case of keep going – KBO, keep buggering on. Isn't that what Churchill used to say during the war?'

As a teenager, Max experienced Britain's post-war recovery. Looking back, he remembers the Fifties. 'In my school, we used to have playground fights – Elvis Presley versus Tommy Steele.' He smiles: that was a world of infinite possibility. For him, it's now a world that's become almost extinct, a loss in his life that's echoed by his condition.

As a Parkinson's sufferer, Max has been growing alert to the smallest signs of ageing. 'I notice that my hair is thinning and that I'm getting what Jacky calls "angry old man" eyebrows. What spooks me more than anything is that while I'm shaving or cleaning my teeth in the morning, I'll find myself stooping until I'm almost bent double. I have to tell myself to straighten up.' He smiles wistfully. 'Straighten up – and fly right.'

☽

Death has been an intimate part of Max's life for several years. When he was in his fifties, he suffered the loss of his wife to cancer and he has spent much time reflecting on fate and mortality. Now, faced with his own endgame, Max is resigned to fighting this battle on his own, and was glad to speak about his inner preparedness. 'It's odd,' he says, 'to use the language of war. How can you fight a battle you know you're probably not going to win? Where the odds are so dramatically against you? Is that even the best way to think about it? It's not a battle, it's a progressive kind of surrender. As English patients, we are so conditioned by the clichés of resistance.'

Max, the stoic, admits he does not quite know how to tell his friends, and dreads the inevitable moment of disclosure. 'They notice I'm slower, and I know they ask Jacky, "Is he all right?"' Max sighs, as if burdened by a heavy weight. 'To begin with, I just didn't want people to know. That's my family's basic instinct. We don't like to talk about personal matters.' He sees his condition, and its progress, as something he has to deal with, but does not want to inflict it on anyone else. Max has a rationale for this approach. 'I don't want to destabilize my family, so it remains an unresolved problem. But now' – he sighs again – 'I'm coming to the point where I think I should perhaps let people close to me know.'

In the ebb and flow of this conversation, we are talking about art, possibly inspired by the lovely Japanese prints on the sitting-room wall. I remember that Van Gogh, in a famous canvas that's now in Boston's Museum of Fine Arts, asked three things: 'Where Do We Come From? What Are We? And Where are We

Going?"* Today, these questions seem rather pertinent. In response, Max concedes that his Parkinson's has not only brought such existential matters into a new and sharper focus, but has also added another poignant query of his own: 'Pessimists say that human life is both horrible and senseless, without meaning. If that's so, then why must we die slowly, as I am likely to do?'

Time: during the endgame, when everything gets reduced to the essentials, Time becomes a priceless commodity, more golden than any corporate handshake or pension. This, I think, is the nub of Max's predicament: like any sixty-something, he recognizes that Time is the one commodity he's running out of. He also knows, in the vaguest terms, how and when his final days might play out: he doesn't want to die slowly. How, I wonder, does he deal with that? Does he have any interest in psychotherapy?

'No.' Max dismisses the idea of counselling with mild derision. 'I mean: what would they tell me?' He refuses to concede weakness, an Ulster Protestant trait. 'I just don't want people to write me off. Do I still feel young? God help me, I think I do, though I am aware of changes emotionally and physically. Perhaps I do look different to people, other than the way I feel.' When Max speaks of his resolve and his future therapeutic strategies, he sounds like a man of resolution.

Max remains a child of war. Memories of austerity

---

* The inscription the artist wrote on his canvas has no question marks, and all the words are in upper case: D'OÙ VENONS NOUS; QUE SOMMES NOUS; OÙ ALLONS NOUS.

linger. Together we recall how, as children, we endured a diet of shepherd's pie, toad-in-the-hole, and fried fish. How, at school, institutional menus featured Spam, corned beef, mountains of lettuce, and 'salad cream'. Kia-Ora orange squash was a juvenile luxury that we both remember, but Max insists with a smile that 'water always came from the tap'. The shadow of World War Two and its colossal slaughter hangs over Max and his generation now as they make their rendezvous with oblivion. Does he, I wonder, defaulting to my 'third thought', think about dying?

'Every day, actually.' Max laughs. 'I'd rather not, but it's unavoidable. In my condition, and at my age, you can't help it. I'm sorting out my will.' He looks round the room. 'Things like who gets the Japanese prints and who gets the contemporary art?' He focuses again. 'Dying?' He pauses in thought. 'I'm not scared of it, though I don't welcome it.'

What does he think dying might be like?

'I haven't got a clue,' he replies. 'Sudden would be good. A quick exit.'

At ease with himself, Max has fulfilled most of his dreams. He has no Bucket List. 'I've been to most of the places I wanted to go to, and done what I wanted to do.' Now he has to make peace with his immediate future. With sequestered thoughts, we share a moment of reflection. 'I've not many regrets. I've had a good life. Perhaps I've fallen short in some ways, but there's nothing I can do about that now. I could have done some things better, but it's too late to make amends. That's the benefit of getting older. I don't feel things quite as intensely, and I have more perspective.'

From art, music, and travel, it's a short step to books. Max is an avid reader. For the Parkinson's patient, literary expressions of the mind and the body in extremis can be therapeutic. In *The Year of Magical Thinking*, Joan Didion writes that 'Grief turns out to be a place none of us know until we reach it.' The same might equally be said of ill-health, and it's a consoling thought.

The end-of-life literature of recent years – *The Black Mirror* by Raymond Tallis; *The Work of the Dead* by Thomas W. Laqueur – suggests that not only will some patients turn to language, but also that language can speak across time and space. Such pain-conscious titles are ones that some patients would never be without.

'Words have a longevity I do not,' is how Paul Kalanithi puts it in *When Breath Becomes Air*. Max and I start to discuss some of our favourite reading from the library of chronic infirmity: Susan Sontag: *Illness as Metaphor* (1978), a series of essays written while she was being treated for breast cancer; Jean-Dominique Bauby's astonishing monologue *The Diving Bell and the Butterfly* (1997); Harold Brodkey's neglected AIDS memoir *This Wild Darkness: The Story of My Death* (1997); Gillian Rose's pocket masterpiece *Love's Work* (1995). For the Parkinson's sufferer, moreover, there is also Michael J. Fox's *Lucky Man* (2002).

It is a suggestive irony that prose rarely pulses with such life as when it grapples with mortality, either in fact or fiction. It's as if we cannot face life's greatest mystery any other way. Some of these graveside testaments seem to speak all the more eloquently because they are whispered from the mysterious antechamber to death. Perhaps the unconscious reasoning behind our fascination with such books is that – we think – we may learn something from words uttered in extremis. Our conversation, circling round, has reverted to the endgame. Now I have another question: would Max, in extremis, accept palliative care for his Parkinson's?

'A hospice?' he queries. This seems like an unwelcome suggestion. 'Of course I'd consider it, though I'd hope it doesn't come to that.' He pauses in thought. 'In that case, I suppose you have to think about your loved ones. It's all very well saying that you want to live out your days at home, surrounded by your family, but that could be an awful burden on other people. You have to balance your wishes against what's being imposed on your family.'

Going one step beyond a hospice, I wonder if he supports assisted dying? Max takes that question in his stride. 'I'm a great believer in people having the right to choose how and when they die, though I'm not sure I'd have the courage to go that route myself. I imagine that, informally, there's still an awful lot of euthanasia.'

Max looks out of the window. From his smile, I guess he's about to indulge a flight of fancy. 'I would love to be like Socrates, and sit on my terrace with a glass of champagne before saying goodbye.' The smile becomes wry. 'I did actually google "hemlock" to see if I could make some at home, but I'm not enough of a botanist.' He chuckles. 'Apparently, it's horribly bitter.' He returns to our theme. 'People have the right to choose their own ending.'

☽

Max is pragmatic about existential matters. On one occasion, referring to his late wife, he observed, very matter-of-fact: 'We act as if death is unusual, when in fact everyone you look at has been touched by it, in one way or another.'

I notice that he seems determined not to be intimidated by mortality. 'I want to work to the end,' he remarks, 'staying as engaged as I can.' He seems happily focused on living in the present moment, the here-and-now, and is debating whether to learn French or Spanish (he already knows Latin). This, he adds, 'is something I've wanted to do all my life.' He admits that he's aware of a time-limit to his 'third age' ambitions, but does not repine. 'I suppose one does tally up these signs of decline, but I don't feel unhappy about that. I'm resigned to my situation, and hopeful that there's still some life worth living.'

I ask him, if he could make a deal with Fate, how many more 'good' years he would settle for?

'Ten.' Max's answer is swift and decisive. 'If I made it to eighty, I'd feel I'd done OK. If I fall short of eighty, I'd say, "That's the cards." I'd rather die a little sooner, than have a long, lingering illness. I think I'd be unlucky not to hit seventy-five, but who knows?'

When, in conversation, he refers to 'Fate' again, I find myself moved by the way Max's 'cards' have fallen lately, and find it impossible not to allude to the irrational workings of an imagined God.

'I don't know what that means,' he replies. 'I'm not especially irreligious, but I don't believe there's a God up there who gives a fuck about me or my life. I mean . . . God isn't going to intervene to cure me. There is no cure for Parkinson's.'

We pause here, as if to acknowledge this brutal and unreconcilable truth, the reality of Max's everyday existence. In a way that I've come to see as typical of the man, Max defaults to optimism again. 'Of course,' he says, 'I will actively seek to delay its progress.'

For a few moments, another silence falls into the room, as we gather our thoughts. Out of nowhere, Max says: 'I feel that the real battle with this thing is yet to come.' Another pause: there's an awful lot unspoken about Max's situation which is, I am quite sure, exactly the way he wants it to be. Just to have had this conversation feels like a small victory in his so-called 'battle'.

So there he is, a veteran, setting out on a long campaign in hostile territory he cannot reconnoitre. On this journey, he will go it alone. That's who he is, a man of courage and gritty determination. I wonder: does he believe in the 'good death' and the art of dying, *ars moriendi*?

'I think I do.' Max perks up at the classical allusion; he has always been interested in the Romans. 'You've given me a very good idea. I'll make it a project. I mean "the End" is staring me in the face now. For decades of your life you can push it to the back of your mind. But now I think about it every day.'

13

THE GOOD DEATH

'The growing good of the world is partly dependent on unhistoric acts; and that things are not so ill with you and me as they might have been, is half owing to the number who lived faithfully a hidden life, and rest in unvisited tombs.'

George Eliot, *Middlemarch*

Later, I discovered that I had wrongly assumed *ars moriendi* to have a classical, Graeco-Roman origin. On closer examination, it turns out to have been a phenomenon from the Middle Ages that may have evolved in response to the horrors of medieval medicine. The original, so-called 'long version', entitled *Tractatus artis bene moriendi*, composed in 1415 by an anonymous Dominican friar, was widely translated, and became much read in England, where the idea of 'the good death' filtered into literature.

As a popular title, *Tractatus artis bene moriendi* was also among the first books printed with movable type, and became circulated in nearly one hundred editions before 1500. This 'long version' survives in about three hundred manuscript versions.

Ars moriendi divides into six parts: the first chapter explains that dying has a good side, and serves to console the terminally ill that death is not something to fear. The second chapter outlines the five temptations – lack of faith, despair, impatience, spiritual pride and avarice – that beset the dying, and how to avoid them.

The next chapter identifies the seven questions to ask a dying man, along with the consolation available to him through the redemptive powers of the Saviour's love. This is followed by a chapter expressing the need to imitate Christ's life. The fifth chapter addresses the friends and family, and outlines the general rules of behaviour at the deathbed. Finally, the sixth includes appropriate prayers to be said for the dying.

Miguel de Cervantes and William Shakespeare both expressed clear views about good ways of going. In the prologue to his final novel, *Los trabajos de Persiles y Sigismunda*, Cervantes likens the impending end of his life to reaching the end of the road after travelling with friends old and new, whom he wishes he could go on conversing with. Shakespeare's understanding of death is polyvalent and all-encompassing. In *Measure for Measure*, the Duke of Vienna, disguised as a friar, instructs:

> Be absolute for death. Either death or life
> Shall thereby be the sweeter . . . .

So too, in *Hamlet*, the student prince articulates a mature and extraordinary mood of resignation:

We defy augury. There's a special providence in the fall of a sparrow. If it be now, 'tis not to come. If it be not to come, it will be now. If it be not now, yet it will come—the readiness is all. Since no man of aught he leaves knows, what is't to leave betimes? Let be.

The lives and deaths of many characters in the *Persiles* also bear out the view that those who live well come to a good end, and those who don't, don't. This was a common attitude. In *The Art of Dying Well*, the Italian Jesuit Robert Bellarmine, a contemporary of Shakespeare and Cervantes, declares, 'True, therefore, is the sentence, "He who lives well, dies well;" and, "He who lives ill, dies ill."' This is a sentiment whose after-life still lingers, leaving questions hanging in the air like gun-smoke after a shooting.

The patient, more than the reader, will be tormented to find that these are questions without answers. Both patient and reader will, inevitably, find themselves in a quasi-spiritual fix. For the writer, at least, there can be a bigger dividend. Words can heal wounds. The consolation that books can offer lies in their courage and their defiance. The exercise of thought, imagination, and creativity can provide real solace. Put words on the page, and you leave a mark behind. But in the process of putting black on white, you might have the sneaking suspicion that you are writing on sand.

Paradoxically, it is from works of the imagination, especially fiction and poems, that we derive the most wisdom about Prospero's 'third thought'. After that anonymous *Tractatus*, post-classical consolatory death literature flourished until the seventeenth century. Other works in the English tradition include *The Waye of Dying Well* and *The Sick Mannes Salve*, culminating in 1650 with *Holy Living and Holy Dying*.

Elsewhere, we find Russian writers doing things that others never dare even to contemplate. Tolstoy's novella *The Death of Ivan Ilych* makes another kind of bleak commentary on 'the good death' that's the equal of Shakespeare and Cervantes. A profound and beautiful meditation on an individual's passing, *Ivan Ilych* is scarcely a hundred pages, but it reverberates like a much bigger book.

☽

This long short story (ninety-eight pages in Aylmer Maude's translation) begins when a certain Pyotr Ivanovich goes to visit Ilych's widow, who describes how Ivan her husband had just died in agony. 'He screamed unceasingly, not for minutes but for hours.' Tolstoy uses this conversation to establish the terror of death, and also 'the customary reflection' of those who are left behind that 'it could not and should not' happen to them. From this stark opening, Tolstoy moves to tell the reader that Ivan Ilych's life, which is narrated in the simplest terms, had been 'most simple and most ordinary, and therefore most terrible'. After a momentary career disappointment in middle age, this unexceptional provincial magistrate gets a new job in a new town, finds a new house, starts to redecorate it, and is perfectly happy.

Then this happens.

Ilych is up a step-ladder, helping his interior decorator with some new curtains, when he slips and should have fallen badly, but manages to save himself. 'It's a good thing I'm a bit of an athlete,' he says. 'Another man might have been killed. I merely knocked myself, just here. It hurts when it's touched, but it's passing off already – only a bruise.' However, despite protestations of well-being, something is not quite right. 'It could not be called ill health', says Tolstoy, with another twist of the narrative screw, 'if Ivan Ilych sometimes said that he had a queer taste in his mouth and felt some discomfort in his left side.'

Eventually, Ivan Ilych goes to see 'a celebrated doctor' and gets drawn into a fog of euphemistic evasion. Tolstoy's account of this consultation is a triumph of irony:

> From the doctor's summing-up, Ivan Ilych concluded that things were bad, but that for the doctor, and perhaps for everybody else, it was a matter of indifference, though for him it was bad.

As his condition worsens, it gets 'rendered worse by the fact that he [Ilych] read medical books and consulted doctors.' At the beginning of Chapter VI, Tolstoy moves to the existential crisis at the heart of the book, summarising Ivan Ilych's situation in two brilliant sentences:

> Ivan Ilych saw that he was dying, and he was in continual despair. In the depth of his heart he knew he was dying, but not only was he not accustomed

to the thought, he simply did not and could not grasp it.

In this crisis, he finds no solace from friends or family, and his worldly desires have faded. All he wants now is the comfort of his loved ones. But they can't understand this, or relate to his suffering. The only person, close to Ilych, who instinctively responds to his master's despair, is Gerasim, his salt-of-the-earth personal servant. Ilych sees that 'no one felt for him, because no one even wished to grasp his position. Only Gerasim recognized it and pitied him. And so Ilych felt at ease only with him.' The inevitable end to the story is as bleak as anything Tolstoy ever wrote. 'What does it mean?' asks Ilych. 'Why? Why must I die in agony?'

In the twentieth century, Sigmund Freud, faced with the complexity of dying, was at once humane, sensible, and profound. 'We must', writes Freud, 'make friends with the necessity of dying'. Death, he instructed, is 'the aim of all life. Everyone owes nature a death.' Freud's own death is one of the subjects in Katie Roiphe's investigation of 'great writers at the end', *The Violet Hour*.

Freud had fled to London, from Nazi-occupied Vienna, in September 1939, suffering from an excruciating cancer of the jaw, for which he had undergone some brutal radiation treatment whose final outcome was a hole in his cheek plugged by a prosthesis he called The Monster. 'My world is again what it was before,' he wrote to a friend, 'a little island of pain floating in a sea of indifference.' Nevertheless, he refused to take any painkiller other than aspirin. 'I prefer to think in torment than not to be able to think clearly,' he said.

An exile, at home in Maresfield Gardens, Freud could rest outdoors on a chaise longue, to enjoy the fading warmth of the autumn sun. Psychologically, he was prepared for the end by the dreadful losses of his middle years. In 1920, when his daughter Sophie died of influenza, Freud had written, 'For us there is little to say. After all, we know that death belongs to life, that it is unavoidable and comes when it wants.' In another essay, he wrote, 'If you would endure life, be prepared for death.' Again, in *Beyond the Pleasure Principle*, also published in 1920, Freud had begun to explore our irrational longing for oblivion, beautifully described by Roiphe as 'the mysterious attraction of undoing oneself'.

The fierce dialectic of life and death persists throughout Freud's work. Famously, he recognizes humanity's profound cognitive dissonance: 'in the unconscious every one of us is convinced of his own immortality.' This is, in other words, an existential conflict we cannot escape. With such thoughts uppermost in my mind, I went to see one of Freud's biographers, the psychoanalyst and writer Adam Phillips.

14

THE NECESSITY OF DYING

'Death destroys a man: the idea of Death saves him.'

E. M. Forster, *Howards End*

A visit to Adam Phillips is an intriguing negotiation, and possibly a quest, or even a voyage into the unknown. I've been going to Phillips' office (formerly his flat) near Portobello Road for about thirty years, but I find it hard to imagine what it must be like to meet him for the first time, still more to have a consultation.

On the appointed day, and at the appointed time, you arrive at Phillips' address. You check your notes. At first, second, and even third glance, it seems highly improbable, even impossible, that this battered off-white door could open a stairway to one of the most sought-after psychoanalytic consulting rooms in London. But it does, and once you press the buzzer marked PHILLIPS, you find yourself climbing, past heaps of junk mail, and dusty household debris, three flights up one of the grottiest staircases in the civilized world.

Today, having reached the top floor, and pausing to look down into the street from the window of the book-cluttered study where Phillips holds consultations with his patients, and does much of his writing, I have no idea how this session will go. We are going to discuss Prospero's 'third thought' as friends, but with the hope, on my side, that I shall acquire some insights into the predicament of humanity in these closing years. After my conversations with Kate, Carol and Max, and my encounters with Professor Lees and Henry Marsh, there's much to explore and digest. But I'm optimistic: a conversation with Phillips is always consoling, and sometimes inspiring. Besides, he's my old friend, and we share plenty of history.

The sixty-two-year-old man who sits opposite me in a small wooden chair by the window, overlooking his street's white stucco, has sometimes, in younger days, had an uncanny resemblance to Bob Dylan, though I must say he is ageing rather better than the author of 'Tangled Up in Blue'. At first, the writer and psycho-therapist steers my enquiries towards conversation by looking away, scarcely meeting my gaze, perhaps be-cause he understands that (if I did not know him better) I might become disconcerted by the awkwardness of his wandering right eye, a childhood trait. He is dressed like a post-graduate in dark corduroy trousers, loafers and a warm brown shirt. On some mornings, he could seem like an inhabitant of Middle Earth; you might also mistake him for a university professor, or even a poet. Somewhere, he has said that he reads psychoanalysis like poetry.

When he talks, he is onto your thoughts very fast, speaking low and urgently, but with great composure, as if he has reflected long, hard and deeply about whatever it is that he decides to vouchsafe. But it's not a sombre dialogue. Irruptions of hilarity are typical, though less so, presumably, during psycho-therapeutic encounters. That remains his private world, which he hugs to himself. If he should ever refer to his many patients, he does so in such an abstract and remote way that there's no loss of privacy.

☽

Phillips has been conducting the intimate exploration of unconscious desires for as long as I've known him. He first came to prominence in 1993 with the publication of an essay collection entitled *On Kissing, Tickling and Being Bored*. Since then he has continued his routine of writing on one, and seeing patients on four, days a week, has published some twenty books, including a short life of Freud, *Darwin's Worms*, *Missing Out* and *Going Sane*, and become both vanishingly elusive, and discreetly celebrated. There was an appetite for Phillips' ironic detachment, and provocative paradoxes. He was taken up by the pragmatic English as a servant of the dark arts who could somehow translate the mysteries of analysis into readable and seductive prose.

As a psychoanalytic writer with practical experience of human beings in extremis, Phillips resists categories. He really doesn't want to be pigeonholed. 'I'm more interested in sentences than ideas,' he says. 'I don't like theories.' He also loves to spin dazzling and epigrammatic lines, for example, 'The unexamined life is surely worth living, but is the unlived life worth examining?'

One way to look at what's really going on in the pages of his books, some of which have been 'in praise of the unlived life', might be to consider Phillips's own career and background.

He was born in 1954, the son of second-generation British Jews of ambiguous Polish extraction who possibly hailed from Omsk. In the Second World War, his father served in a tank regiment in North Africa, and won a medal. My own father served with the Royal Navy in the Pacific; if he ever spoke of this experience, it was to joke about his mundane service medals. Reflecting on this, Phillips and I turn to talking about the aftermath of two world wars, a subject of great mutual interest, which he describes, poetically, as 'a kind of haunting'.

In my quest into the mystery of life, death, and the endgame, this seems like a good place to start. Phillips observes that 'this haunting takes many forms. In the immediate aftermath of conflict, there's an extraordinary transition from states of fear and exhilaration to the routines of civilian life. Having a family and raising children in peacetime took place in a highly disturbed emotional atmosphere.'

Phillips goes on: 'For those who survived, the war was incredibly exciting and really unrecoverable from. There's a radical incompatibility between wartime and peacetime existence. Coming home from the war meant adjusting to the fact that the rest of your life was going to be incredibly boring.' At the same time, the wartime generation had learnt to adjust to separation, isolation, and loss, and – something they would try to pass on to their children – to not feeling hurt when you were hurt. Our parents had equipped themselves for conflict, according to Phillips, by 'self-anaesthesia'.

This, a dominant motif in post-war British life, only added intensity to the project of rekindling the Self that began in the Sixties and reached its full flowering in the Nineties. The traumatic dividend of the Second World War, Phillips concludes, left demobbed veterans of both sexes obsessed by varieties of loss or grief. They were, he suggests, 'either envious of people who had fought in the war; or no longer found life worth living, and identified with the dead; or felt they were living a kind of "death-in-life"; or would ask obsessively, "Where's the excitement?"' On this analysis, he contends that the British fixation on symbols of loss and grief translates into the national sponsorship of 'third thoughts'.

Phillips, swerving away from the aftermath of war, describes a happy career at the cathedral school in Cardiff, spending, he says, 'more of my childhood than I would have liked sitting under Epstein's *Christ.*' He admits that he 'wasn't a reader until I was thirteen or fourteen'. In place of books, Phillips says he was chiefly interested in 'my friends, sport, and Nature'. The young Phillips was obsessed with birds. 'I don't know why,' he adds, in a rare moment of personal bafflement, 'but the *National Geographic* was my pornography.' With an aviary in the garden, he kept humming birds, parrots, sunbirds, quail, tanagers, and bananaquits. He begins to laugh at the memory. 'It was a hell of a lot of birds. I really learned to read because I wanted to read about birds.'

English literature, meanwhile, was becoming the other passion of his adolescence. He read everything: D. H. Lawrence, the Metaphysicals, Donne, Pope, Conrad, Blake, the Romantics ... So where did the psychoanalysis come from? Here, Phillips describes something like the experience of a vocation. 'I can remember being in Bristol – aged sixteen or seventeen,' he replies, 'and I bought a copy of Jung's autobiography, *Memories, Dreams and Reflections*. I read this, and I thought, "This is what I want to be."'

And so he was. Phillips trained as a psychotherapist under Masud Khan, a Freudian course of instruction. 'Khan was wonderful for me,' he says. He breaks off to recall an occasion when he missed the start of a session, and Khan mischievously observed, 'I'm not going to say the obvious things about being late, except that you won't be late for your own death.'

Timing is everything. He had started his analysis at the end of a period, the 1960s and 70s, dominated by R. D. Laing, when psychoanalysis was prestigious, but by the mid-1980s psychoanalytic writing had become academic and turgid. Speaking to Paul Holdengräber in the *Paris Review* (2014), Phillips remarked:

When I started in psychoanalysis—in British psychoanalysis—it was a very earnest and sentimental profession. There was a kind of vale-of-tears attitude to life, with the implication that life was almost certainly unbearable, that the really deep people were virtually suicidal, and it was a real struggle to believe that love was stronger than hate.

I hardly ever came across an analyst, when I was training, who made me feel that they really loved sex. So it was very difficult to be a relatively happy person training to become a psychoanalyst.

It's time to talk about what Freud, in a famous essay on *King Lear*, once called 'the necessity of dying', and to explore what this might mean in relation to the experience of getting on in life. When, I ask, did Phillips first have an apprehension of death?

'As a boy, I can remember driving up to see my grandparents,' he replies, 'when a magpie smashed into the windscreen. I was absolutely devastated, and I can remember saying, "The magpie will never be alive again."'

Phillips seems to hold the memory up to the light. 'It was as if I had an idea of extinction,' he goes on. 'At that moment, my childhood fantasy was "There'll never be another magpie", and that felt absolutely devastating. As I look back on it now, it feels as if it was about something being absolutely irretrievable and beyond my control. I felt totally helpless, as though something had gone for ever.'

I wonder: was he frightened? 'In memory,' he replies, 'it feels like a devastation but – thinking about it now – it must have been extremely frightening.'

As a boy who kept tropical birds, Phillips was certainly aware of death in relation to the creatures he kept, but the shock of the magpie's death was unprecedented. 'No one I knew, or in our family circle, died until I was in my adolescence.' Since then, at home and at work, he has learned to negotiate the experiences of loss and grief.

His father died fourteen years ago, having been diagnosed with bowel cancer and given three weeks to live. Now the 'nameless dread' had morphed into a mood that was more philosophical. 'On one occasion,' he reports, 'after my mother had told me he was not expected to survive the night, I went down to Cardiff, and found my father sitting up in bed, reading the newspaper.' His father told him, 'Last night, I dreamed I was dying, and it was an incredibly *voluptuous* pleasure.' Phillips repeats the phrase, savouring its resonance.

There were some more false alarms and then, he says, 'When I wasn't there, he did die.' He adds, 'I didn't think of saying goodbye because I felt – and feel – that our relationship is ongoing. He's still very present to me,' he concludes.

Something of the father's serenity seems to have been passed on to the son. Phillips volunteers another, more recent memory – of his own near-death experience. He describes driving down the motorway with his partner, the professor of fashion Judith Clark. 'The car starts going like this – ' he gestures with a rolling movement of his hands ' – and then, quite suddenly, it became clear to both of us that the car was out of control, and we were going to die.'

He pauses to let this information sink in. 'And it was just fabulous.' A smile. 'It was one of the most ecstatic, intense experiences either of us has ever had.' Phillips goes on, 'What actually happened was that the car turned over six times, landed on its wheels, and we lived.' Another ironic smile. 'So: a miracle. But then there was a helicopter, and we were taken to Swindon hospital, where we were put in this room with very low light. And we both thought we were dead. We had this genuine experience that we'd actually died and were in an afterlife. Because of the dim lighting it was all rather filmic. We were just lying there and it was extraordinary. I suppose we were in shock.' He stops in mid-flow to reflect on the memory. 'As we talk about it now, I think of death as a relief and a release, or as an experience that is not an experience.'

For a moment, Phillips the psychoanalyst places this fragment of autobiography in a professional context. None of his patients cease fretting about The End, he explains, but now wonders, 'Why can't we be Eastern about this, and just stop worrying about letting go . . . ?'

Out of nowhere, I find myself recalling Lisa Jardine, a mutual friend, who died recently from breast cancer. There's a pause in the conversation. 'She was seventy-two,' observes Phillips. We both look at each other, with the same thought. Yes, maybe we've only got ten years. After sixty, the passage of time gets easier to calibrate: a half-century is a comprehensible unit of time. We, who have been friends for more than thirty years now, know what ten years might feel like.

'Loss and mourning is integral to our development,' Phillips says. 'Death is at the heart of psychoanalysis because the psychoanalytic life-story is plotted in terms of loss, which is often described as "a kind of death". In my work, after my training as a child psychotherapist, I have seen so many people who have been profoundly disturbed by deaths in the family.'

We return to Freud. Making friends with 'the necessity of dying', says Phillips, is a very optimistic statement, for Freud. 'If we're going to love realistically,' he goes on, 'we have to acknowledge transience – the full spectrum from pleasurable experiences to people actually dying.' Here he quotes Henry James: ' "The real is that which it is impossible not to know." ' Among his patients, Phillips believes that the death is always hovering offstage in every conversation.

'At each stage of the life cycle,' he says, 'everyone is preoccupied by it, even if they don't always speak about it.' He notes that there's a great fear of oblivion with patients who have 'a feeling of not having lived. Some people want to mourn the death of a life that never happened.' This is one of Phillips' favourite themes. I remember, on another occasion, his observation to me that 'life is the lives one doesn't have'. He also likes to quote the poet Randall Jarrell's remark that 'the ways we miss our lives are life'.

As a stroke survivor, occasionally I can find myself mourning the life I've lost. Like any survivor, I have had to practise functioning from day to day free from the bitter taste of regret. One benefit of the ageing process, and the onset of the endgame, is that we acquire some forward-looking preoccupations, possibly unwelcome, but nonetheless replete with anticipation.

I ask Phillips if he has a private, internal age, to which he replies, 'If we'd had this conversation when we were forty – and perhaps we did – I'd have said thirty. But now, for the first time, I do feel my age. And I like it because I find it genuinely interesting.'

☽

Phillips is fully engaged with the world. For himself, there is the daily routine of seeing private patients, and writing every Wednesday. He has three children, two girls and a boy; and his partner is a curator of dress at the London College of Fashion. 'Like everyone else,' he says, 'I just have to live from day to day, taking one step at a time.'

I'm not surprised that he disputes the cliché summary of advancing years. 'I don't think ageing is the loss of youth. Ageing is ageing. Every stage of the life cycle is potentially interesting. And it's particularly interesting if you don't think of it elegiacally, if you don't think, "What have I lost?" but instead, "What can I do now?" There will be more possibilities when we are seventy.'

This is a response echoed by the American playwright Wallace Shawn, who observed in a recent interview that 'one of the nice things about the life of writing is that as you get older, you're suddenly different and you make use of that in your work. And that's quite nice because, for a lot of people, getting older and changing can be a sad experience that doesn't provide that many benefits.'

Phillips agrees that the changes associated with age sharpen his focus on life. 'Choices become more imperative, and the question of what we are going to do with our time becomes more urgent now that we know it's not infinite. Being much older means that you are again dependent – but now you're an adult. No one has ever been that dependent, except as a baby. But as a baby you're not that sentient. Old age gives us the first conscious experience of being dependent.'

In the twenty-first century, modern medicine will resist the tide of almost any disease with antibiotics. Yet this does not always satisfy the needs of the elderly. Atul Gawande has addressed the discontent felt by those undergoing life-saving treatment towards a medical profession that treats the human frame while neglecting its mind and consciousness. 'We've begun rejecting the institutionalized version of ageing and death,' writes Gawande, 'but we've not yet established our new norm. We're caught in a transitional phase.'

For many people, this 'transitional' aspect of old age becomes a struggle. Unreconciled to ageing, they conduct an undignified masquerade of youth that never fails to be ridiculous. This, inevitably, is an operatic rendering of the cognitive dissonance we bring to the endgame. But, of course, making friends with the 'necessity of dying' is sometimes little short of a miracle. 'It's amazing,' says Phillips, 'how much people will put up with. We say that life is sacred, but life can also be hell.' In his long essay *Darwin's Worms*, he expresses this resilience more eloquently: 'People's capacity to survive loss and even devastation is at once a banal and remarkable fact. We can't help but be amazed by what people live through.'

I observe that Hell is a literary and imaginative convention, to which he replies, 'Books are one of the ways we think about death and dying.' Phillips and I talk for a moment about the literature of death and dying. We both share a love of *Death In Venice*. Thanks to Visconti's film, Thomas Mann's short novel comes, as it were, with its own soundtrack, the Adagietto from Mahler's Fifth Symphony. The movie has a simplicity the novella resists, but Mann's long story, which is set against an epidemic of cholera, is haunting and profound. The moment at which Gustave von Aschenbach crosses the lagoon to la Serenissima subtly evokes the transportation of the dead to the underworld:

> He had a feeling that something not quite usual was beginning to happen, that the world was undergoing a dreamlike alienation, becoming increasingly deranged and bizarre . . .

Mann's story, like all stories surrounding the imminent deathbed, strikes both of us as consoling. In summary, Phillips draws his own conclusion: 'Conversations and literature: that's how we acquire the language appropriate for dying. Once you have fallen out of a religious sensibility,' he goes on, 'you are a bit marooned. We've got medical language for the physiology of dying, and religious language for the meaning of dying. But in the middle there's a void.' Reflecting on that 'void', I wonder: 'Do people who are dying, in your experience, think about a "good death"?'

Matter-of-fact, he replies: 'I think we all fear a degraded, painful end. Most people would probably describe it as hopefully pain-free, surrounded by a loving family.'

At this reference to hospices, Phillips becomes quite

animated. 'Hospices are really interesting places,' he observes. He recalls one of his former patients who wrote to say he was dying in a hospice. 'Could I come and see him? So for six weeks I saw him once a week, and it was an extraordinary experience.'

'How extraordinary?'

'Well, in the first place you are with a group of people who are definitely dying. And in the second place, people in hospices are often left to themselves. So they are, as it were, alone in their own delirium. I found I was having a different kind of conversation. It was as though I was interrupting this man's dream. He was certainly talking to me, but he was very much in his own world.'

'Was it therefore pointless?'

'No, it was the exact opposite. It was very definitely worth it for me, and it was imperative for him. He really wanted to talk about his relationships with two women in his life. Things that he felt ashamed of, regretful about, and enraged by. Things he had never been able to articulate before.' Phillips, who has now been in conversation for more than an hour, pauses to add, 'He didn't want to die with things unsaid about personal matters that had, as it were, been set aside.' This patient had been, it turned out, a man in love with two women. 'He wanted an internal resolution.'

In a moment of free association, something pops into mind, and I find myself referring to *The Death of Ivan Ilych*, the little book I've been carrying in my pocket for weeks. As we talk about Tolstoy, I recall a passage from the opening of *Darwin's Worms* in which, considering Darwin and Freud, Phillips writes:

> [They] thought of themselves as trying to tell the truth about nature, and nature was what the truth was about. One could only understand human life by understanding its place in nature. And the three truths they took for granted about 'Man' were: that Man is an animal, that he must adapt sufficiently to his environment or he will die, and that he dies conclusively. They both declared, in different ways, the death of immortality.

Crucially, for that all-important reconciliation with the 'third thought', Phillips locates the thrill of human experience, and the meaning of life in the ephemeral nature of being:

> After the death of God, it is transience that takes up our time. Nature is careless with 'her' creations. She is endlessly fertile, but to no discernible end. One couldn't believe in Nature in the way that one could believe in God . . . Whatever it is now that sustains life does not seem to care about its quality. Suffering is only a problem for us.

Phillips goes on to quote Wallace Stevens, 'The brilliance of the earth is the brilliance of every paradise'. Stevens decides that 'one can only write poems of the earth, as Darwin and Freud did, if one is happily convinced that there is nowhere else to go.' In a powerful conclusion, he writes that 'When transience is not merely an occasion for mourning, we will have inherited the earth.'

In the project of inheriting the earth, the quest for a new language for the pragmatic reconciliation of life and death, and ways of living and dying, must take us into the universe of the imagination – into fiction. The greatest novels inspire a kind of dream in which thoughts and feelings, memories and experience blur within a cathedral of language: Herman Melville's *Moby-Dick*, for example; or Marilynne Robinson's *Gilead*. Much more compressed, but equally brilliant, are several short novels which make perfect bedside reading. Joseph Conrad, *Heart of Darkness*; Muriel Spark, *The Prime of Miss Jean Brodie*; Robert Louis Stevenson, *Dr Jekyll and Mr Hyde*; and F. Scott Fitzgerald, *The Great Gatsby*. Even in extremis, humanity retains a narrative gene: it's to myths and stories we must inevitably return.

Works of literature fill the void of faith, but in the end, everything goes pear-shaped. The best-laid plans fail. Trust in good health gets betrayed. Futures go south. Rational projections spin awry; families implode. Chance, fate, old age, mortality, and finally oblivion take over. Bereavement cuts through the hopes of the living like a scythe.

With no certainties, the mundane details of everyday behaviour become a relentless improvisation. Religion falters; and optimism self-destructs. Personality disintegrates under the merciless shell-fire of fear. Confronted with the whirlwind of contingency, the human animal, reverting to type, hunkers down. Adam Phillips' vision is right: under this bombardment, it is remarkable how humanity finds the resilience to cling on. And it will be words and language, the thing that makes us human, that will be sustained to the end.

15

LAST WORDS

'It is profoundly interesting to know what the mind can still contain in the face of apparently certain death.'

George Orwell

Writers and their last exits occupy a special place in the literary imagination. Ever since Plato described his mentor's noble death in *The Last Days of Socrates*, the conduct of that ultimate farewell, so enthralling to readers, has become a mini-genre: Henry James, on his deathbed, referring enigmatically to 'the distinguished thing'; Freud refusing drugs stronger than aspirin so he could think clearly, before finally choosing the moment of his own death; John Updike, ready to give up, putting his head on his typewriter, because it was too hard to type up his final poems about dying, but then finding the strength to finish them anyway; and David Bowie, almost teasing at the end, writing of 'the next stage'. In *The Violet Hour*, Katie Roiphe acknowledges the mystery implicit in this subject: 'It would be hard to pin down why I chose these particular people' – Susan

Sontag, Maurice Sendak, Dylan Thomas et al. 'I was drawn to each one of them by instinct, felt some heat coming off their writing, some intuition that they could answer or complicate or refine the questions I was asking myself.'

In *Henry the Fifth*, Shakespeare makes a famous and unforgettable nod to the fascination of such memorials in Mistress Quickly's account of Falstaff's passing:

> He parted just between twelve and one, even at the turning o' the tide – for after I saw him fumble with the sheets, and play with flowers, and smile upon his finger's end, I knew there was but one way. For his nose was as sharp as a pen, and he babbled o' green fields. How now Sir John? quoth I. What, man! Be of good cheer. So he cried out, God, God, God, three or four times.

Mistress Quickly, a practical Englishwoman of robust temperament, has no use for the consolations of faith; besides, she loves 'Sir John' and can hardly bear his loss:

> Now I, to comfort him, bid him that he should not think of God. I hoped there was no need to trouble himself with any such thoughts yet. So he bade me lay more clothes on his feet: I put my hand into the bed and felt them, and they were as cold as any stone; then I felt to his knees, and they were as cold as any stone, and so upward and upward, and all was as cold as any stone.

Falstaff's appeals to 'God' go to the heart of the deathbed scenario. And yet, at the end, with no possible postponement of the inevitable, there is only the enigma of faith. In a secular world, God and his comforts are strikingly absent for most people, but ideas about an afterlife still hover, like spectres, in the human imagination.

In the hunt for clues to this mystery, 'last words' have a special place in the human imagination. A flash of wit, perhaps, or a last flourish of wisdom? Who knows? On learning that he was mortally ill, the Scottish philosopher David Hume wrote a short autobiography, *My Own Life*, a valedictory personal account inspired by his final days:

> I now reckon upon a speedy dissolution. I have suffered very little pain from my disorder, and what is more strange, have, notwithstanding the great decline of my person, never suffered a moment's abatement of my spirits . . . I possess the same ardour as ever in study, and the same gaiety in company.

Was it Hume's studied equanimity that piqued James Boswell's curiosity? Did the obsessive biographer hope that the rendezvous of a great mind with the unfathomed vastness of eternity would inspire some special insight into the unknown? Certainly, he was an incorrigible nosy parker. So, in the summer of 1776, Boswell went to visit Hume on his deathbed. Literary ambulance-chasing has its macabre side. Boswell's report of that last meeting is a classic of slightly creepy reverence, a kind of superior voyeurism:

On Sunday forenoon, the 7 of July, being too late for church, I went to see Mr David Hume, who was returned from London and Bath, just a-dying.

I found him alone, in a reclining posture in his drawing-room.

He was lean, ghastly, and quite of an earthy appearance. He was dressed in a suit of grey cloth with white metal buttons, and a kind of scratch wig.

'He seemed to be placid and even cheerful,' noted Boswell. 'He said he was just approaching to his end. I think those were his words.' Boswell knew that Hume was a confirmed atheist, and he wanted to investigate his state of mind. Had there been any last-minute reconsiderations? A late return to faith, perhaps? 'I know not how I contrived to get the subject of immortality introduced,' he confessed. In Boswell's telling, Hume's response was robust and well-sourced:

He said he never had entertained any belief in religion since he had begun to read Locke . . .

I asked him if he was not religious when he was young.

He said he was, and he used to read *The Whole Duty of Man*; that he made an abstract from the catalogue of vices at the end of it, and examined himself by this, leaving out such vices as he had no chance of committing.

Boswell, the biographical bloodhound, continued his reportage: Hume then said flatly that 'the morality of every religion was bad', and, added, in deadly earnest, that 'when he heard a man was religious, he concluded he was a rascal.'

Boswell continued:

> I had a strong curiosity to be satisfied if he persisted in disbelieving a future state even when he had death before his eyes.
>
> I was persuaded from what he now said, and from his manner of saying it, that he did persist. I asked him if it was not possible that there might be a future state. He answered that it was a most unreasonable fancy that we should exist for ever.

As the great atheist in his grey cloth suit, with his 'lean and ghastly demeanour', began to enumerate his objections to the possibility of an afterlife, Boswell faithfully recorded every detail:

> That immortality, if it were at all, must be general; that a great proportion of the human race has hardly any intellectual qualities; that a great proportion dies in infancy before being possessed of reason; yet all these must be immortal; that a porter who gets drunk by ten o'clock with gin must be immortal . . .

Boswell then asked the philosopher the big question: Did the thought of approaching annihilation ever give him any uneasiness? Unfazed, Hume answered: 'Not the least; no more than the thought that he had not been . . .'

> 'Well,' said I, 'Mr Hume, I hope to triumph over you when I meet you in a future state; and remember

you are not to pretend that you was joking with all this infidelity.'

'No, no,' said he. 'But I shall have been so long there before you come that it will be nothing new.'

Boswell admitted that he had conducted this conversation in 'a style of good humour and levity', but he was unrepentant.

Perhaps it was wrong on so awful a subject. But as nobody was present, I thought it could have no bad effect. I however felt a degree of horror, mixed with a sort of wild, strange, hurrying recollection of my excellent mother's pious instructions, of Dr Johnson's noble lessons, and of my religious sentiments and affections during the course of my life.

Boswell, puzzling over this brush with greatness and its meaning, wrote: 'I could not but be assailed by momentary doubts while I had actually before me a man of such strong abilities and extensive inquiry dying in the persuasion of being annihilated.' Finally, switching to a more elegiac mood, Boswell recalled an old memory of Hume that's at once vivid, candid and revealing:

He had once said to me, on a forenoon while the sun was shining bright, that he did not wish to be immortal. This was a most wonderful thought.

Not only had Hume's deathbed come to resemble a debating chamber, this scene is a reminder that death, in the past, was much wittier than our own heavily sedated exits. To another visitor, who asked the great atheist if he would not finally renounce the Devil and all his works, Hume is reported to have replied, drily: 'Sir, now is not the time to be making new enemies.'

☽

There is something pleasantly garrulous about Hume's last exit. In the twenty-first century, the imminent death we are grappling with does not encourage conversation, but it does not let up, either.

Today, in a more secular society, the best end-of-life writing often has a quasi-journalistic inspiration. Christopher Hitchens, who died too young at sixty-two, challenged his fate in *Mortality*, which was published posthumously in 2012. Hitchens first announced his condition (oesophageal cancer) in *Vanity Fair*, with a series of despatches from the place he called 'Tumourville'. Similarly, Oliver Sacks reported his slow last exit in several moving pieces for the *New York Times*, posthumously collected in a short volume, *Gratitude*. Paul Kalanithi, a gifted neurosurgeon struck down in his thirties by lung cancer, planted the seed for *When Breath Becomes Air* in a *New York Times* op-ed article, 'How Long Have I Got Left?'. It's the pitiless reality of this final stretch that all we have got is: questions.

2015–16 was a memorable year for departures, a reminder of Philip Roth's verdict in *Everyman* that 'Old age isn't a battle; old age is a massacre'. It began with the passing of Oliver Sacks towards the end of summer, on 28 August 2015. Just before he died, aged eighty-two, Sacks composed some last words, a valedictory piece entitled 'Sabbath':

And now, weak, short of breath, my once-firm muscles melted away by cancer, I find my thoughts, increasingly, not on the supernatural or spiritual, but on what is meant by living a good and worthwhile life—achieving a sense of peace within oneself.

Soon after Sacks' death, Svetlana Alexievich won the Nobel Prize for Literature. She remarked that 'Life is beautiful, but too short, dammit.' She added, coolly: 'The fairest thing in this world is death – no one has ever managed to buy himself out of it.' A few weeks later, Lisa Jardine died, and then Philip French, the *Observer*'s film critic.

As the year turned, this 'massacre' continued with the deaths of David Bowie, and the actor Alan Rickman, both aged sixty-nine. Neither had ever seemed old to me: Bowie had composed the sound-track to our lives in the Seventies; Rickman had been a benign and constant presence on stage and screen. His death was another memento mori.

Towards the end of January, the publisher George Weidenfeld died, and then Terry Wogan (a colleague said, 'We thought he was immortal,' a line stolen from P. G. Wodehouse on the death of his daughter Leonora).

In March, there was more annihilation: the deaths of the magician Paul Daniels, the novelist Anita Brookner, and then the comedian Ronnie Corbett, who passed away on the same day as the architect Zaha Hadid.

With the coming of spring, all these deaths seemed abstract enough. People die all the time. But then, it suddenly became personal. Idly surfing the net one day, I discovered – to my considerable astonishment – this entry:

'Robert McCrum, obituary' published in the state of Maine, USA.

Needless to say, I hastened eagerly to catch up with my own demise:

> Saco & Mars Hill – Robert Phil McCrum, 69, passed away Monday, December 21, 2015 at Mercy Hospital surrounded by his loving wife and children. Born on May 7th, 1946, Robert was raised in Mars Hill by Phil and Doris McCrum. He is a graduate of Aroostook Central Institute and attended the University of Maine. He married his high school sweetheart, Jennifer (Craig) McCrum, on June 23, 1966.

What a good American my doppelganger seemed to be: the vice-president of his company; a member of the National Guard; a devoted son and father; and a faithful husband who, I read, 'loved traveling with his wife and family'. Every detail of his obituary felt like a not-so-subtle rebuke to another Robert McCrum. According to the *Saco Times*, my double 'was a great example of a Christian husband, father and grand-father.' That was not all; he was fun to be with, too. 'Robert had a great sense of humor, knew when to listen and when to offer advice. He is survived by his wife of 49 years'. By this point in the obituary, I was hating them both. Besides, their news was too close to home. Was there no respite? As if to ward off evil spirits, I began to doodle an A–Z of ill-health drawn from among friends and associates.

A has just had a perilous operation to remove her gall bladder; B nearly died from a blood infection associated with routine knee surgery; C is having extensive dental treatment to save her adult teeth; D lately died in agony after a short illness; E has just emerged from a severe nervous breakdown; F is on his deathbed, with cancer of the pancreas; G has endured two years of excruciating bone transplants to repair a shattered leg; H has advanced Parkinson's; J has just suffered a *coup de vieux*, ageing ten years in two; K is battling with his father's Alzheimer's; L is having chemo; M continues to suffer from multiple sclerosis; N is no longer blind, but still cannot read a computer screen; O suffers from geriatric depression; P has leukaemia; Q dropped dead while carving the Sunday roast; R has incipient dementia; S has his head in a brace, having broken his neck in a bicycle accident; T is drying out in a clinic; U had his heart broken, lost the will to live, and died from a massive coronary; V is dying of ovarian cancer; W is in a nursing home, having survived an attack of sepsis; X is in a hospice; Y is seeing oncologists; and then there's Z, aged twenty-five, who is as fit as a fiddle, with not a care in the world. Perhaps Z has the most to worry about.

Mr Reaper, meanwhile, was not letting up. The following week, in April, it was the turn of Arnold Wesker (eighty-three), Victoria Wood (sixty-two), and Prince (fifty-seven). At the end of that month, the novelist Jenni Diski died from cancer. The other literary deaths of 2016 included Henning Mankell, Harper Lee, and P. D. James.

As spring turned to summer, the press reported the deaths of the writer and journalist Sally Brampton, the entertainer Caroline Aherne, the film director Michael Cimino, and the poet Geoffrey Hill. All these deaths were described with hardly a reference to their subjects' last words. This is new: before modern medicine anaesthetized the deathbed, that last exit was often quite conversational. Today, such valedictory dialogues are so exceptional they can become media phenomena.

The BBC correspondent Steve Hewlett, who died in February 2017 from oesophageal cancer, was a journalist and broadcaster who used a year of fatal illness to extraordinarily moving effect, articulating his struggle in print and on air. Not only did Hewlett write a must-read cancer diary in the *Observer*, he conducted an unforgettable series of intimate conversations with presenter Eddie Mair on BBC Radio 4.

'Two men talking about cancer' became essential listening, while Hewlett tackled his diagnosis and subsequent treatment with a journalist's thoroughness. He demonstrated how to fight illness, never flinched from researching his condition on Google, widening the circle of his enquiry to talk to friends who had been through cancer, investigate the best treatment, and challenge his doctors.

Millions responded to these broadcasts. Steve made himself his own story out of a profound commitment to hard-nosed reporting, as well as a deep humanity: 'I'm absolutely convinced that the more we talk about cancer – both to our families, friends and loved ones – the better it is for all concerned,' he said. 'Above all it's empowering for them.' And consoling for him.

A baby-boomer, born in 1958, Hewlett was, in his final year, coming to address the questions that trouble the generations who have been raised to believe they can enjoy lives of infinite possibility: why am I here ? what is my fate ? where am I going ? As a great correspondent, he did this, quite practically, by reporting on his cancer with painful and unflinching candour, never hinting at self-pity.

Hewlett's answer to the conundrum of life and death was wise and existential, and highly articulate. With wry good humour and supreme matter-of-factness, he suggested to his audience that ageing is as natural as breathing. Steve filled the void left by the death of religion and the collapse of faith, to give his untimely exit a sense of ritual and a language appropriately expressive of our need for consolation. In so doing, he conducted a master-class in the noble art of dying well. And he did it, extempore, from what became his death-bed.

Is the silence of the contemporary endgame not medicine's most discomforting side-effect? More urgently, in 2016, the enemies of the terminally ill are the social media by which everything gets publicized. Some will say that Facebook and Instagram offer comfort, and perhaps they do. Only the bereaved can tell us if the new accessibility of death is a consolation or a curse. Jenni Diski, who was terminally ill for two years, made her own, dry commentary on this race to the end in her posthumous memoir:

> If it were a race, the first man home would be Oliver Sacks with Henning Mankell a close second. Lisa Jardine won a race of her own, staying shtum publicly, her death a surprise except to the few who knew. So Clive James and Diski still battle it out for third place . . . It's a delicate balance, this publicising of one's cancer.

In Gratitude became the perfect symbol of this 'delicate balance': it was published in the very week of her death. Not even Diski's Cambridge neighbour, Clive James, could have orchestrated such an exit.

16

ONE FOOT IN THE GRAVE

'I do not fear death. I had been dead for billions of years before I was born, and had not suffered the slightest inconvenience from it.'

Mark Twain

The curious case of 'the late Clive James', defying gravity at home in Cambridge, is almost as singular as Hume's provocative exit. In the summer of 2013, on news of his failing health, the world's press gave James the last rites: valedictory interviews, hushed bulletins, and a posse of shiny blonde Australian TV anchormen and women flying to his doorstep.

These global obsequies turned out to be premature. Clive James did not die, and when I went to visit him in Cambridge on 3 July 2013, on behalf of the *Guardian*, as one of many media Boswells, I could not put the nosy Scotsman's curious enquiries out of mind. The Australian writer is not David Hume, but there were some mundane parallels.

I probably knew James as well as Boswell knew Hume, which is: well enough. Over thirty-something years we have exchanged intermittent conversations. Literary acquaintances, even associates, we weren't strangers either. We had shared publishers; occasionally, we'd had dinner. When Sarah published *The Anglo Files: A Field Guide to the British*, her account of living in Britain as an American journalist, Clive had been a generous supporter of her work. Indeed, he had declared, in a witty conclusion, that she would 'be hailed as one of England's supreme analysts, preparatory to her being executed on Tower Green.'

Few expats know more about the strange, and sometimes baffling, quirks of English life than Clive James. Ever since he landed here in the icy winter of 1962, he has been engaged in a raucously entertaining argument with our national habits. Like many post-war Australians, James came to Britain to get closer to the source of a literature with which he was mildly obsessed. He claims he was simply joining the herd. 'I did it because everyone else did,' he told me. 'And when I got here I ran out of money. It was sixteen years before I had enough money to get home.'

The convivial, chimes-at-midnight Clive became notorious for trailing his cultural coat with exquisite references to Pushkin and Mallarmé, 'The Ballad of Reading Gaol', allusions to Freud and Mandarin poetry, and snatches of Ovid and Catullus. In the process, he virtually invented TV criticism at the *Observer*, infuriated the poetry establishment, and reminded the British reading public what could be done with the English language if you had been raised in the Sydney suburbs and had the good luck not to go to Eton or Winchester.

In short, he found a voice. In its prime, there was nothing else quite like it.

The best of James's observations – for instance, that 'Perry Como gave his usual impersonation of a man who has simultaneously been told to say "cheese" and shot in the back by a poisoned arrow' or that Arnold Schwarzenegger in *Pumping Iron* resembled 'a brown condom filled with walnuts' – had an unequalled, surreal hilarity that, in the words of one awestruck disciple, made 'your brain yelp with delight'.

Clive James became celebrated, parodied, acclaimed, patronized, lionized, and disparaged – high and low – but never ignored. In his newspaper days, he was Sunday's must-read column, a vertiginous mix of literary exuberance, show-off allusion, topical wisecracks, and fuck-you Aussie irreverence. By the mid-70s Clive had become that literary phenomenon, as rare as the hippogriff, a critic who might put Rambo and Rimbaud in the same sentence, and somehow get away with it. In fact, he'd probably done that already, and you hadn't noticed, being too dazzled by his comparison of *Beowulf* to *Jaws*.

So when, during his 'last summer', I travelled up to Cambridge to interview him about his magnum opus, a new verse translation of Dante's *Divine Comedy*, I was unsure of the outcome. There'd been rumours that he was at one end of the home stretch, and I more than half expected to find him at death's door. But the old fellow who welcomed me into the terraced house off Chesterton Lane was the same incorrigible Clive with that wicked, conspiratorial smile and sardonic *bien être*.

He was moving slowly in slippers, racked with emphysema, coughing badly, and needing oxygen, but putting his best face on adversity. As well as his admission to intensive care, he was now dwelling in a kind of internal exile: estranged from family, from good health, even from his own native land. His circumstances in old age – James was then seventy-three – evoked a fate that Dante might plausibly have inflicted on a junior member of the damned.

His health had lately got so bad that he had been obliged publicly to deny a viral rumour of his imminent demise. Possibly he found rejuvenation in the macabre satisfaction of reading rave obituaries from fans. If word of his death had been exaggerated, there was no question, on meeting him in 2013, that he was into injury time.

'Essentially,' he said, as we settled into the spartan living room of his two-up, two-down terraced house, 'I've got the lot. Leukaemia is lurking, but it's in remission. The thing that rips up my chest is the emphysema. Plus I've got all kinds of little carcinomas.' He pointed to the place on his right ear where a predatory oncologist had recently removed a threatening growth. 'I'd love to see Australia again,' he said. But he dared not venture further than three weeks away from his local hospital. 'That means I'm here in Cambridge.' With a vintage display of Anglo-Australian stoicism, James celebrated his incorrigible vitality, quoting the words of the Merrie Monarch, Charles II, about taking 'an unconscionable time to die'.

☽

Since then, however, reports of his death had become steadily less credible. As if he had been energized by his stay of execution, his conversation, and his literary output, continued to fizz with wit and wisdom. Just before I began to write *Every Third Thought* in the late summer of 2015, I went to see him again. He was about to publish another book – *Sentenced to Life*, a collection of poems – and had some more things he wanted to get off his chest.

'The end is nigh,' he said, opening his front door to greet me again, 'but not that nigh. My obituaries were so fabulous,' he twinkled, in a preliminary gambit, 'that I felt more or less obliged to walk the plank.' Back in 2013, believing he was virtually defunct, he had cooperated with the media's obsequies, and watched himself being 'safely buried'. But then, in a cartoonish twist of fate, he didn't die, after all: he was the Comeback Kid from Kogarah, NSW. It was, he had to concede, with creditable sheepishness, 'all a bit embarrassing'. At home in a house full of paperbacks and NHS palliatives, this latest conversation defaulted to his afterlife, a subject he treats with sardonic merriment. 'I've got a lot done since my death,' he remarked, paying tribute to his doctors. He gets his immune system rebuilt every three weeks through a process of immuno-globulin enhancement. 'It's quite restful. I sit there all afternoon. I can read a book, and even write something, while they pump in stuff through a tube.'

I was fascinated to explore the creative dividends of writing with one foot in the grave. This late surge in output is not unprecedented, but many writers half his age and twice as fit would be thrilled to be so productive. As well as publishing his verse translation of *The Divine Comedy*, a collection of essays, *Poetry Notebook: 2006–2014*, with other volumes already in the pipeline, he has made so many 'farewell appearances' (first in London and then in Cambridge) that his friend P.J. O'Rourke had advised him to 'soft-pedal this death's door stuff because people will get impatient'. There had been just one problem with this game-plan, however: its star player.

Clive Vivian Leopold James had not yet wearied of himself. Far from it. For James, his trips to A&E were an alarm call that perked him up no end. He responded to finding himself in extremis with all the equanimity of a drowning man. Above all, he got serious. 'I am restored by my decline', he writes in *Sentenced to Life*, 'And by the harsh awakening that it brings.'

Ever since 1958, Clive James has always written poems that exhibit a strong bias towards entertainment. 'The Book of My Enemy Has Been Remaindered' is a classic of light verse. In old age, fulfilling his claim that he is 'a late developer', he found a big subject, possibly the biggest, his own last exit. The best blooms from this late flowering, collected in *Sentenced to Life*, were older, sadder, and wiser, the work of a clown who has found his circus inexplicably dark.

James, however, remains an Australian 'larrikin' with a megaton of inner resource. His glass is never less than half full. He divides his poems into 'lovelies' and 'funnies'. In *Sentenced to Life*, there are just two 'funnies', cabaret turns, 'about death, doom, and destruction'.

This, the Boswell in me discovered, was as close as he would get to the difficult questions surrounding oblivion. More typically, his title poem ('Sentenced to Life') describes 'a sad man, sorrier than he can say', who confesses that 'my sin was to be faithless' and who describes seeing himself afresh 'with a whole new emphasis', something perilously close to regret:

> What is it worth, then, this insane last phase
> When everything about you goes downhill?
> This much: you get to see the cosmos blaze
> And feel its grandeur, even against your will,
> As it reminds you, just by being there,
> That it is here we live, or else nowhere.

Montaigne once observed that we laugh and cry at the same thing, and James has been an old master at playing both sides of the street. 'Japanese Maple', which went viral in 2013, caused him some embarrassment, he says. 'The poem more or less promised that I would only live till autumn. But then autumn came – and there I still was, thinking, "Shucks!" ' The lyrical maple sapling, meanwhile, has matured into a sturdy young tree, happily flourishing in his back yard.

Another potential source of awkwardness in his highly public endgame, to which he seems to have become well attuned, is the curse of sentimentality. How does he deal with that? 'You can't deal in feelings without running the risk of being sentimental,' he instructs, and then spins a brilliant summary. '"Sentimental" really means "an excess of feeling without sufficient cause." I think there's plenty of cause in my work.'

That's an explicit reference to the central theme of *Sentenced to Life*, the poems written to his wife, Prue Shaw, the dedicatee of the collection. This theme in the book already came with a health warning. When we met in 2013, husband and wife were estranged and James, who had misbehaved badly with another woman back in Australia, was in the middle of a campaign for reconciliation with Prue which, characteristically, he conducted in print. Some of the best poems in the new collection were for her, again. 'Balcony Scene', riffing on *Romeo and Juliet*, closes with this appeal:

> Be wary, but don't brush these words away,
> For they are all yours. I wrote this for you.

James's valedictory melancholia is a powerful source of inspiration. Speaking of the poems addressed to Prue, his friend Tom Stoppard observes: 'One of the most moving chords ever struck in English literature is the sound of a man falling in love with his wife.' When I embark on a tactful exploration of this marital mine-field, I soon discover that the poet himself has his own splinter of ice firmly in place within. 'There's a dilemma,' he says. 'I hope that she [Prue] is pleased, and I hope she likes them. But finally the poet writes for himself. I think that what Prue likes about my poems is that they are written for myself.' A mischievous chuckle. 'Maybe she thinks my "self" has improved . . . !'

☽

The phone rings. It's Addenbrooke's Hospital booking him to check the wound on his scalp. 'This stuff happens all the time,' he says, seeming temporarily lowered by the intrusion of medical concern.

A beat. 'I'm a natural inhabiter of the limelight,' he continues, explaining his ability to work so close to extinction. Surely, at this late stage, he must have a choice about how to live in these final days? 'That's the strange thing. I got confined to – ' he gestures round the kitchen in which we are sitting – 'to my burrow, but the lights haven't been switched off.' He perks up again. 'It's very gratifying. The condition of most writers is to be forgotten, and while they're alive, too. That must be tough.' He preens irrepressibly, comparing himself en passant to Madonna. 'Luckily, I'm a story.'

I imagine that the incorrigible Boswell would ask if he fretted about posterity, but James is already onto that one. 'Posterity?' he challenges, with a kind of spooky intuition. 'It's here and now. I've always thought that it was here. If you play to the gallery, that's posterity. The best you can hope for is another gallery after you've gone, but you won't see it. Statistically, it's unlikely that much of what one does will be read for ever. It may just be one or two poems.' He defaults to another joke. 'My "Japanese Maple" poem is famous among people who own a Japanese maple.'

Clive James's appetite for the limelight is only a small part of the explanation for the show he's putting on in his final years. He is too steeped in the classics to be ignorant of 'the Art of Dying'. *Sentenced to Life* contains a poem of homage, 'Compendium Catullianum', whose title was cooked up for him by his neighbour, the classicist Mary Beard. From memory now, he begins to recite some of Catullus' 'Carmen 101', written in memory of the poet's dead brother, which inspired his own poem.

Multas per gentes et multa per aequora Vectus
advenio has miseras, frater, ad inferias,
ut te postremo donarem munere mortis
et mutam nequiquam alloquerer cinerem.

'It goes on,' he says, 'to that famous last line, "*atque in perpetuum, frater . . .*"' He glances out of the window towards the Japanese maple in the garden. '*Ave atque vale.* I learned a lot of Latin poetry here,' he says. 'That's the great thing about a place like Cambridge. So many great minds. It's like being in Los Alamos.'

In the closing poem of *Sentenced to Life*, he admits himself to be 'dying by inches'. This, more than the ironic bravura of his most recent platform appearances, seems to represent the real Clive James, a writer whose commanding voice contains a constant variety of colour and tone. Regretting his frailty, he has become, he says, 'the echo of the man you knew.' Death, as much as love, is perhaps the poet's truest inspiration. 'I think I'm writing better now than I ever did. That's where lyricism comes from. The love lyric is always full of approaching sadness.'

In retrospect, on the train back to London, I wondered if I had not hoped for one last, definitive exchange here that would have nailed the posterity question once and for all:

Me: You've lived so long, and defied the odds so well.

CVLJ: I have.

Me: Do you ever have fantasies of immortality?

CVLJ: My work will be immortal.

Me: All your work?

CVLJ: My poems, novels, songs – don't forget my songs. Let's face it. Prose is for drongoes. The love lyric is the supreme form of literary self-expression.

Me: I like that.

CVLJ: Of course you do. That's Clive Vivian Leopold James in a nutshell. Your supreme Australian writer.

Me: Here's to your immortal memory.

CVLJ: Hey, that's not original.

Me: No, but it's a good one.

CVLJ: Fair dinkum.

Clive James never admits this – why should he? – but he burns with the will to live, and its corollary, a determination not to be forgotten. Almost wistful, he returns to talking about Australia, 'the land of my youth, the land of permanent youth. I think about that all the time.' Putting aside, if he can, this area of regret, there's the relentless tick-tock of failing health. At least he's in no pain. 'What I've got doesn't hurt. I've been lucky. I don't know if I could concentrate if I was in pain. I've never had to stop.' I'm impressed by Clive James's refusal to leave the stage without several curtain calls. In his own show-off way, his response to a highly exposed endgame has been generous and dignified.

A small silence intercedes. 'What will happen when I go?' he wonders aloud, possibly for my benefit. 'I don't know.' He pauses. 'I'll be glad to be remembered at all.' Another pause. 'I've seen some very gifted people destroy themselves.' A final pause. 'I've had a lucky life. That includes five years I didn't expect to get.'

Meanwhile, awaiting his next rendezvous with Addenbrooke's, he is reflecting on all the fine words that 'poets and philosophers have used to mark the path into the killing ground.' His own last lines from 'Sunset Hails a Rising' run on:

> No supernatural powers
> Need be invoked by us to help explain
> How we will see the world
> Dissolve into the mutability
> That feeds our future with our fading past:
> The sea, the always self-renewing sea.
> The horses of the night that run so fast.

As I prepare to say goodbye, Clive comes up with a valedictory line that leaves David Hume in his dust: 'You can always say that you're on your last legs, but the way you say it might equally suggest that you can run a mile in your socks.'

17

STARING AT THE SUN

'It is not death, it is dying that alarms me.'

Montaigne

Last night, I spoke to M about a mutual friend who was, she said, 'not very well', a euphemistic phrase freighted with unspoken anxiety. On the many approaches to the grave, language absorbs a lot of our sorrow. In the course of this year devoted to 'third thoughts', I've noticed a declension in our conversations about the old. We start out by saying so-and-so has 'had to see a doctor' or 'has been having treatment'. Then we might say that we hear so-and-so is 'on the mend', or is perhaps 'having tests'. If things turn out not to be 'fine', we'll report that X or Y is 'in a bad way', or even 'looks frightful'. This can open the floodgates. When we spoke last night, after a few moments of discretion, M suddenly said, 'You know that they've stopped treatment. B says he's dying . . .'

According to La Rochefoucauld, 'Neither the sun nor death can be looked at steadily.' With half-closed eyes, we can try, but not even the remorseless intrusion of routine mortality can ever quite prepare you for the thing itself, that death in the family, or the unexpected loss of a colleague. I have an image in mind that, at such moments, death becomes like an indifferent electrician switching off the lights in the deserted stadium of the human soul.

'There is nothing you can do', writes Nora Ephron. 'Nothing. Everybody dies. Death is a sniper. It strikes people you love, people you know, it's everywhere.' When the human hourglass runs out, it is one experience of ageing to become progressively more familiar with the dramas and rituals of death and dying. It's certainly the end of the road. My friend, K, a popular novelist, says that her tombstone will have this simple inscription: 'Finally, a good plot.'

As we approach these final moves in the endgame, it's as well to be prepared for what's in prospect, even if we know that this experience is likely to be as strange, disturbing and unpredictable as life itself. The *Guardian* of 3 February 2016 published a moving account of one typical British death:

> My father spent 10 days dying. He was 84 and he had lost his wife – my mother, whom he adored, and without whom he felt life was a lot less worth living – three years earlier. He died of old age, and it was entirely natural.
>
> The process, though, did not feel that way at all, at least not to me. Dad had been bedridden for months and was in a nursing home. He stopped

eating one day, then started slipping in and out of consciousness. Soon he stopped drinking.

For 10 days my sister and I sat by his bedside, holding his hand, moistening his lips. Slowly his breathing changed, became more ragged. During the last few days, the tips of his fingers turned blue. His skin smelled different. His breath gradually became a rasp, then a rattle.

It sounded awful. We were sure he was in pain. The doctor reassured us he wasn't; this was a human body dying naturally, shutting down, one bit at a time. We had not, of course, talked about any of this with Dad beforehand; we had no plans for this, no idea of what he might have wanted. It would have been a very difficult conversation.

The doctor said he could give him something that would make him at least sound better, but it would really be more for us than for my father. 'My job,' the doctor said, 'is about prolonging people's lives. Anything I give to your father now would simply be prolonging his death.'

So we waited. When it finally came, death was quite sudden, and absolutely unmistakable. But those 10 days were hard.

Humanity's association with death can become strangely therapeutic. Another resonant irony: the contemplation of mortality can re-enfranchise older patients into a world of feeling from which, through prudent self-protection, they may have become detached. In Donne's bleak formula, expressed in Meditation 17 of

Devotions, 'No man hath affliction enough that is not matured and ripened by it.'

As I renewed my scrutiny of life in extremis, I returned to a familiar moment in the endgame – the conduct of palliative care. I found myself, as a moth to a flame, drawn back to the Cambridge hospice I had first visited as long ago as 1993, and written about in *My Year Off*, as the guest of the then medical director Dr Tim Hunt.

Arthur Rank House is a pleasant single-storey pale-brick building tucked away in the grounds of Brookfield Hospital, on the edge of Cambridge city centre. In a new century, it's easy to forget the contemporary revolution in attitudes to our mortality. At first, when it was opened in 1981, the hospice was the object of prejudice and fear. Neighbouring households, who were spooked by the idea of death and dying on their doorstep, demonstrated against it as a health risk, protesting that the inmates and their ambulances would be contagious. Thirty years on, there's a new battle to be fought: some local residents are up in arms against the building of a mosque. While Islam was reaching Cambridge, the hospice movement came of age. There is now a national association (Hospice UK), and Arthur Rank House is just completing the process of moving to a £10.5 million purpose-built facility in the Gog Magog hills, on the outskirts of Cambridge.

Today, however, I am returning to the old building, marvelling anew at the cheerful informality of its atmosphere. Such kindly and relaxed warmth, in stark contrast to the chilly realities of death, must come from deep inner resources: friendly smiles are a vital bulwark against tides of darkness.

As I waited to meet the chief executive of Arthur Rank, I watched one very sick old man in pyjamas, slumped in a wheelchair, being pushed into reception by his elderly wife. The patient was breathing with great difficulty and wore a breathing tube linked to an oxygen supply. There was a mad, almost feral, look in his bloodshot eyes and his white hair was wild and wispy. I blurted out a 'Good morning', but his response was barely intelligible. He seemed to be in pain, and I could hardly suppress the thought that he might be better dead. One glance at his long-suffering wife was enough. I was reminded of the recent passing of another old friend; his doomed, rearguard action against leukaemia; and his final days in a London hospice. It was a relief to be ushered away to meet Dr Lynn Morgan, the executive head of Arthur Rank, and the person responsible for steering this multimillion-pound business.

Lynn, formerly a government employee with the National Lottery, actually joined Arthur Rank as a direct result of her own father's death, an exit with its slightly comic side. 'In the end,' says Lynn, 'my dad died from kidney failure. But by that time, he'd got virtually everything, and had survived four aneurysms.' She smiles at the memory. 'He used to say that Arthur Rank saved his life.'

I quickly discovered the explanation for this paradox: some years ago, her father had been admitted into intensive care, where he was not expected to survive. 'They were going to switch off the life-support system,'

Lynn explained. 'As a family, we had agreed that this was the humane thing to do. So we went away to take a break, and have a coffee, but when we came back there was a new shift and a different doctor, who said, "Maybe not yet. Let's do some more tests."'

'After that,' she continued, 'he was transferred to Arthur Rank in the expectation that he would die within a couple of weeks. When he was first brought in here, he had nothing to live for. I remember seeing him in a foetal position, and he was only eating half a yoghurt a day. But, as soon as he arrived, they gave him a spa bath, to freshen up, and he began to come back to life.'

Now Lynn is laughing. 'He just got better and better.' Eventually her father left the hospice and had two or three more years of useful life, while Lynn re-evaluated her work as a government servant. 'I thought if I'm going to work really long hours, why shouldn't I do something that didn't feel so futile?' she says. Soon after this modest epiphany, she applied for the post of CEO.

Lynn Morgan's team is led by Lorraine Petersen, the director of medical services, and Liz Webb, who runs the clinical side. The improvised informality of Arthur Rank's beginnings are a thing of the past. Tim Hunt, who had been such a charismatic and controversial presence here twenty years ago, is long retired, but his intuitions about our final days and his exploration of the taboos surrounding the deathbed deserve to be re-membered. 'For people who are terminally ill,' he once told me, 'things can be much blacker than they need to be. They expect to die tomorrow, or the next day. They see Death just around the corner. They can't sleep. How can you expect someone, even a healthy person, to feel well in the day if they don't sleep at night? No textbook will tell you this. Patients will tell you. It's because they have a fear of dying in the night, of not waking up.' Years ago, in the National Hospital, I had found this to be true for myself. Some of my best and worst thoughts were those I had during the excruciating solitude of a sleepless hospital night. As a former patient, I remember mistaking the light under the door in the darkness for the beginning of dawn, only to discover the bedside clock reading 02:30.

From experience, I understand now that, during the endgame, we default to resilience, perfecting a cognitive dissonance in which we entertain contradictory thoughts: part of us knows, and accepts, that we are dying but another part feels and thinks that we still have a future. In 'Considering the Alternative', Nora Ephron puts it this way: 'Death doesn't really feel eventual or inevitable. It still feels . . . avoidable somehow. But it's not. We know in one part of our brains that we are all going to die, but on some level we don't quite believe it.' In one of my conversations with Henry Marsh, he had once observed that it's 'as though our brains are hard-wired for optimism. A good doctor will speak to both these dissonant selves, neither lying nor depriving the patient of hope, even if it's only the hope of life for a few more days.'

A pioneer in the hospice movement, Tim Hunt also taught that, contrary to popular belief, the terminally ill do not want crowds of visitors. 'Husbands and wives,' he used to say, 'have a tendency to call relatives home for deathbed farewells. Actually, dying is a lonely business. The dying just want one person with whom they can share the silence and the darkness – a companion.' The aim of the hospice movement is to facilitate a gentle transition to a state of solitude and acceptance that will make the lonely moment of passing as comfortable as possible.

☽

In any hospice, there are many practical considerations, mixed with matters of life and death. Part of its function is to help supply a narrative for those who are reaching their end. The staff encourage their patients to make plans, with memory boxes, family mementoes, and so on. They see their job as all about supporting the patient as they make their exit, but will insist that 'it's not one route in, and one route out'. While Lynn and I sit chatting over coffee in the deserted day room, her colleague Liz Webb begins to describe the hospice routine which, she says ruefully, 'is never routine'. Unsurprisingly, palliative care requires emotional stamina. 'We work with staff to manage stress,' she remarks. 'There would be a high degree of burn-out if we did not take care of our nurses. We offer a lot of support to the staff, with access to counselling 24/7.'

Arthur Rank also makes an impressive commitment to an everyday expression of sympathy. 'What we try to do is make the process more humane,' Liz explains. 'We have a micro-grant scheme for our patients and their families. Sometimes, a small amount of money can make a real difference. For instance, we had a young Polish family here the other day. They had no money, and no support network. After the father's death, we arranged for his wife to take a Ryanair flight back to Poland to drop her youngest child off with his grandparents. Then she flew straight back to Cambridge for her husband's funeral.'

I wonder about the limits to care, and the pressures on beds, and ask: would they turn away a patient with dementia – someone who might live on for months, or years?

'No.' Both Liz and Lynn firmly resist this suggestion. 'We never exclude anyone. We look at every case on a clinical and individual basis.'

How to make dying as calm and comfortable as slipping into another room is a bigger question. On the deathbed, questions of faith and belief jostle in the mind with worries about 'the job of living' and the 'journey of life'. This, in turn, reflects the timeless contrast of complexity (life) vs. simplicity (death). In those final days, approaching Shakespeare's 'mere oblivion', we are 'sans eyes, sans teeth, sans taste'. Walking past the wards, some of the bed-ridden, terminally-ill figures I glimpse through a half-open door are incontrovertibly 'sans everything'.

One of the most fundamental questions that every hospice nurse has to deal with is: 'How long have I got?' Tim Hunt's approach, still widely used, is to dispel the apprehension of ignorance. 'You cannot say,' he once remarked to me, 'that "You're going to die in three or six months." It's highly disturbing to do that. If you do that, the date gets marked in the diary.' Since those days, there's a new hazard for the hospice nurse: Google. For the terminally ill, the temptation to google a) your diagnosis and b) your life expectancy can be overwhelming.

Bigger than 'When?' or 'Where am I going?' is the question of 'How?' Here, mercifully, the hospice movement can offer reassurance. Most patients will die in their sleep, a deeper and deeper sleep. At Arthur Rank, it's usually a question of coming to terms with an imminent journey. Several patients who come into the hospice will be sent home. Almost half the intake – 40 per cent – will not stay for long. It will be their wish to go home to die. This will be a decision reached in consultation with the patient's loved ones. There is now an impressive body of literature to assist families in extremis. Elisabeth Kübler-Ross's groundbreaking *On Death and Dying* identifies five stages of dying, popularly known by the acronym DABDA:

1. Denial — The initial reaction. In this first stage, individuals believe the diagnosis is somehow mistaken, and cling to a false, preferable reality.
2. Anger — Patients become frustrated, especially with loved ones and nurses. Typical psychological responses during this phase would include: 'Why me? It's not fair!'; 'How can this happen to me?'; 'Who is to blame?'; 'Why would this happen?'
3. Bargaining — Here, the negotiation for an extended life is made in exchange for a reformed lifestyle.

4. Depression — Patients say things like: 'I'm so sad, why bother with anything?'; 'I'm going to die soon, so what's the point?'; 'I miss my loved one, why go on?' They become saddened by the probability of death. Some individuals may refuse visitors and spend much of the time silent, mournful and sullen.

5. Acceptance — The common response becomes: 'It's going to be okay', combined with 'I can't fight it, I may as well prepare for it.' Individuals now embrace mortality and their inevitable future.

Paul Kalanithi was a model for this final stage. He writes: 'I'd suspected I had cancer. I wasn't taken aback. In fact, there was a certain relief. The next steps were clear: Prepare to die. Cry. Tell my wife she should remarry, and refinance the mortgage. Write overdue letters to dear friends.'

There are so many exit strategies. Liz Webb says: 'Some patients never want to be told bluntly that they are dying. Then the nurses and doctors have to work out how to respond. Other patients want to know exactly.' It's as if, on their approach to the hospice, everyone's arrival reflects their character and preferences.

'Sometimes,' adds Liz, 'patients will make the transition to an acceptance of death in the ambulance on the way here. We are always clear that coming here is about dying – we are all dying, of course – but our motto is: "Making Every Moment Count". Western society sees death as a failure. We aim to help our patients live every moment that's left to them, hopefully with as much pain relief as possible.'

Dr Lorraine Petersen, Arthur Rank's medical director, joins our conversation, speaking dispassionately about her work and its needs. 'There are some difficult cases,' she says. 'You have to eyeball the patient. It's not the family's decision. There are,' she concedes, 'some things we can't do. Some things are done more safely down the road in Addenbrooke's [Hospital]. If there's going to be too much monitoring involved, we'll say no. But we'd rather say yes, and then assess.'

Once again, I recall my encounters with Adam, Carol, Henry, and Max. I have been impressed by their near unanimous determination about the assertion of human rights. More and more people today insist they want to choose the moment of their extinction. In the last two decades, the 'Right to Die' movement has become more vociferous. Within the Commonwealth, Canada has just passed a bill legalizing 'assisted suicide'. We can never know the torments of a life made unbearable by dementia, or cancer, or paralysis. So I ask: 'What about assisted dying?'

A loaded pause interrupts the conversation. I sense that no one here really wants to entertain this difficult subject. Eventually, Liz replies, speaking carefully. 'Some patients will wish to have conversations with our doctors about that.' Another pause. 'Our doctors will have this discussion, but always on the basis that assisted dying is illegal in Britain. The doctors will talk through with the patient what it is that makes them want to take that route.'

Ultimately, many of these discussions at Arthur Rank – indeed, anywhere in the UK – can only ever be about exploring options of pain relief and controlling anxiety. The final decision rests with the patient. Liz Webb says firmly: 'If our patients choose to seek assisted dying, that's the point at which they must make their own arrangements.'

'Meaning?'

'They will have to go to Switzerland.'

18

THE DYING OF THE LIGHT

'In vain do individuals hope for immortality, or any patent from oblivion, in preservations below the Moon.'

Sir Thomas Browne, *Urn Burial*

In his fiction, Terry Pratchett, who was never squeamish about mortality, made 'Death' a character. At the end of his life, grappling with Alzheimer's, he became a passionate advocate of the right to choose, challenging what he saw as the 'questionable' assumptions of those who assert that no one need consider a voluntary death of any kind, when better end-of-life care is always available. He condemned the suggestion that 'affliction is somehow a penance for an unknown transgression', railed at 'the choreographed outcry' against assisted dying, and scorned 'the British tradition of bullying from the top down: the common people are stupid, and we who know better must make the decisions for them.' In a fierce, rhetorical peroration to his article, 'Assisted Dying: It's time the government gave us the right to end our lives', Pratchett wrote:

The common people are not stupid. They might watch god-awfully-stupid reality TV, but they are very clever about the politics of blood and bone and pain and suffering. They understand about compassion and they are nothing if not practical about these things.

In preparation for my hospice visit, and the urgent question of the 'Right to Die', I had already spent some time with the novelist Salley Vickers, who lives a few miles from Arthur Rank House, on the other side of Cambridge. Her recent novel, *Cousins*, is set in the university, and is about Will, who suffers locked-in syndrome. Will explores assisted dying, and finally persuades his cousin Cecilia to help him.

This is a subject close to Vickers' heart. She has always said, quite openly, that if she becomes incapacitated in old age (she is now in her sixties), she will not hesitate to take her own life as expeditiously as possible. 'Oh yes,' she exclaims, 'I would *absolutely* advocate assisted dying.'

She has good reasons: 'My family history is rife with Alzheimer's. My mother had Alzheimer's; her mother had Alzheimer's; my mother's brother had Alzheimer's; and so on. I have to make sure I can scuttle off. Yes: I definitely have the means – oh most definitely – and, if it comes to it, I'm going to go that way.' She has no intention of putting her children through the torment of caring for a parent with Alzheimer's. Indeed, she wrote *Cousins* partly because she believes that people should have the possibility of dying when they choose.

As our discussion turned to the question of how easy, or difficult, it might be to kill yourself, I recalled my conversation with Henry Marsh, a passionate believer in 'patient autonomy' and the kind of 'doctor assisted suicide' performed in some parts of the USA. Both Marsh and Andrew Lees have memories of the euthanasia practised in British hospitals up until the 1970s. This involved successive injections of potassium chloride, diacetylmorphine (heroin), and finally suxemethonium. 'I have no illusions about what dying from a brain tumour might be like,' said Marsh, at one of our meetings, 'though whether I'd have the courage to take my own life, I don't know.'

Dying – the fact of death – is simple enough: we run out of air. Throttled of oxygen, the heart stops; in the subsequent blackout, the brain-stem is murdered with the speed of an expert strangler. In *How We Die*, Sherwin Nuland gives a succinct description of the universal processes that we'll all experience as we die: 'The stoppage of circulation, the inadequate transport of oxygen to tissues, the flickering out of brain function, the failure of organs, the destruction of vital centres – these are the weapons of every horseman of death.' Now, driving away from Arthur Rank House, I crossed Cambridge to complete my conversation with Salley Vickers, whose resolute coming-to-terms with death and dying I have known for years.

Vickers occupies a Victorian terrace house in a quiet cul-de-sac. We talk at length over cups of coffee in her large light kitchen-diner, hung with paintings and bunched cuttings, from the fine old bay tree you can see through the French windows. 'How,' I ask her, sitting by the green Rayburn, 'how do we reconcile the conflict between medical progress and that necessary friendship with the reality of death and dying?'

As I'd hoped, Vickers has a clear answer: 'I suspect the concept of "progress" in all areas tends to make a craving to control the terms of life seem more possible and thus more of a right,' she says. 'Medical advances are no exception. We are not well trained in the stoicism of our forebears, stoicism being less attractive than hedonism, but none the less a valuable attribute.' Her voice drops. 'I have never been afraid of dying (though plenty afeared of ageing). I've always regarded death as a tragedy for the survivors rather than the subjects.' A characteristic flash of irony. 'Of course that might all change when I am balanced on the edge about to topple off.'

'Well then,' I persist, 'has your family accepted your stated intention of "taking steps" to end it, if there's no hope? Have you had any argument from them?'

'I've only confided to one of my children,' Salley replies. 'He understands about the Alzheimer's threat but emphatically wants no part in it.' His mother might secretly have to acknowledge that response. For Vickers, a Christian, there must be something 'God-given' about our allotted span of three score years and ten. Meanwhile, as the evening light creeps in across the Fens, I am still wrestling in my mind with this 'right to die'.

'So,' I ask, 'is it a right?'

A long pause supervenes. Finally, Vickers says, 'Yes, I think it is a right.' She hesitates in thought. 'It's an odd right, because we don't have the right to be born. So maybe we don't have the right to die.' She sighs at the weight of the question, and comes up with a pragmatic response. 'This is what you'd call a tricky area, and it's certainly an individual matter.'

'Like faith?'

'I do think that religion does help, though not in the old-fashioned sense,' she replies. 'Nowadays no sensible religion (except possibly Islam), and certainly no sensible Christians, really believe in Heaven and Hell. But religion gives you a sense that something will survive, a memory in other people's eyes.'

I am about to mention ritual, and the benefits of being part of life's narrative, both its plot and sequence, when Salley adds, 'Religion gives you a drama in which you play a part, and being part of a drama offers a great compensation. I mean, death is dramatic, and if you have religion it gives the drama of death a place in a theatre of things.'

When I suggest that, at the end, religion supplies an essential narrative, Salley carries the thought forward: 'It gives you a story, and once you have a story or a drama you become more important. It really doesn't matter if it's true or false. It's much more comforting to have it. I think this is where Pascal is so right. We might as well bet on there being a point to the whole thing. Why not? It makes a better story.'

'Pascal's wager', to which Vickers referred, starts from the assumption that the stakes are infinite if there is even a small probability that God does in fact exist. In that case, Pascal argues that a rational person should live as though God exists, and seek to believe in God. If God does not actually exist, such a person will have only a finite loss (some pleasures, luxury, etc.), whereas they stand to receive infinite gains (for instance, eternity in Heaven) and avoid infinite losses (for example, eternity in Hell).

The pragmatic outcome of Pascal's wager is that most people live according to the precepts of a faith they have never believed in. At the end it will be the language of their adopted religion that carries them towards oblivion. For Richard Dawkins, a celebrated atheist, in that extreme condition, many of us will take refuge in a 'personal' idea of God. He is, says Dawkins, 'an imaginary friend', which links to Salley's candid assertion that it's immaterial whether our religion is true or false. It works because we believe it. That, in turn, connects to our fear of the unknown. It's often said that many people only turn to religion 'because they are afraid of death'.

From Pascal (1623–1662) it's a short step back in time to one of my favourite writers on this subject, Montaigne (1533–1592). 'If I were a writer of books,' the latter remarks at one point, 'I would compile a register, with a comment, of the various deaths of men: he who should teach men to die would at the same time teach them to live.' As a writer of essays, Montaigne has plenty to say about humanity's approach to death and dying, and especially the fear of death: that most intense of all emotions. He contextualizes his own work by observing that 'Philosophizing is nothing other than getting ready to die' and asserting the wholesome nature of his endeavour, 'one of virtue's main gifts is a contempt for death'. This must be a good step towards a mature consideration of death and dying. In *Grief Works*, Julia Samuel, a veteran grief counsellor, explores the necessity of coming to terms with grief and the emotions associated with loss. Samuel writes, in words which echo my own argument, that 'Our culture is imbued with the belief that we can fix just about anything and make it better; or, if we can't, that it's possible to trash what you have and start all over again. Grief is the antithesis of this belief: it requires endurance, and forces us to accept that there are some things in this world that simply cannot be fixed.'

Finally, Montaigne's advice is practical: 'We know not where death awaits us: so let us wait for it everywhere. To practise death is to practise freedom. A man who has learned how to die has unlearned how to be a slave.'

19

THE NOWNESS OF EVERYTHING

'Things are both more trivial than they ever were, and more important than they ever were, and the difference between the trivial and the important doesn't seem to matter. But the nowness of everything is absolutely wondrous.'

Dennis Potter, *Seeing the Blossom*

It's approaching midsummer. There's a storm thundering overhead; and I am listening to Rachmaninov's 'Elegy', op. 3 no. 1, composed in a frenzy, just days after the death of Tchaikovsky. It is a melancholy, passionate, and thrilling piece whose notes are torn by grief. This music always sounds cathartic, but there are many other composers whose chords will reconcile extremes of feeling. As Terry Pratchett puts it, 'With Thomas Tallis on my iPod, I would shake hands with Death.'

In the search for narrative, the first motive of all writing, I find classical music especially helpful in establishing a mood for the quest. My soundtrack to *Every Third Thought* includes: Tallis's *Spem in Alium*; Bach's unaccompanied cello suites; Barber's Adagio for Strings;

Beethoven's late string quartets; Mozart's *Ave Verum Corpus*; and from Purcell, 'When I am laid in earth', Dido's Lament in *Dido and Aeneas*; or from Rossini, his *Petite Messe Solonelle*, described by the composer as 'the last of my sins of old age' (*péchés de vieillesse*). Maybe it is fanciful to attribute special insights into the human condition from composers in their final days, but it remains a potent fantasy.

Music offers a language often more powerful than prose, but I cannot read a score. Words are my medium, so I come back to print and paper. Everyone has their favourite literary distraction: poetry, short stories, even crosswords and children's books. In *The Ministry of Fear*, Graham Greene acknowledges the potency of the first books to seduce our imaginations: 'No later books satisfy us like those which were read to us in childhood – for those promised a world of great simplicity of which we knew the rules.' The need for clarity towards the end might be a reason to return to *Alice in Wonderland* or *Charlotte's Web*. When I was convalescent at the National Hospital in 1995, Sarah used to read aloud to me, after the heat of the day, from her favourite E. B. White, in the dusty gardens of Queen Square during those late summer afternoons I associate so powerfully with the aftermath of my 'brain attack'.

Twenty-something years ago, on my return from hospital, I found myself reading the King James Bible for the music of its language and the thrilling arrests of its narrative. Here was a cathedral of words whose expression of faith had no meaning for me, but whose sonorous periods can make you weep. I cherish the mystery of that response. The demons of inner dread can inspire a search for friends and allies, while patients can find solace in the strangest juxtapositions of words and music. Some will turn to the potency of musicals; others to Mozart or Wagner. Words can be harlequins or priests, and good words offer their own kind of covert resolution. Next to the childhood classics we love, there are the books which share with the reader an insight into the experience of being in extremis.

I know from the letters and emails I still receive about *My Year Off* that readers get a thrill from the special intimacy with a book that offers previously unexplored truths about the extremes of life and death, the regular grist to the mill of confessional writing. 'Life-writing', observes Blake Morrison, an old master of this genre, 'turns out to mean death-writing', which is another way of saying that we want truths about mortality (which we cannot know) more than truths about everyday life (which we know too well).

As much as a craving for morphine, the patients' need for authenticity in prose becomes a kind of addiction. In hospital, where everything is at stake, the next question becomes: 'How true is it?' To which the paradoxical answer is that, while it does not always have to be true in a literal sense, it must be intrinsically honest. That's to say (because, after all, any memoir is *composed*), it might be deliberately shocking, or calculatedly confessional, or cynically manipulative, or even self-dramatizing, but it must express a fundamental truth. Rousseau's *Confessions* are often provocative, absurd and preposterous, but they speak the man, and we believe them. Without that trust, the contract between the reader and the writer breaks down. When that happens, the words fly up meaninglessly into nothingness. To the agony of the patient's solitude, as described by Donne in *Devotions*, there's no worse cruelty than empty words.

Sometimes, only poetry can speak to such agony: favourite passages from Shakespeare, Wordsworth, Hardy, Yeats, and Eliot. Any selection will depend on the unbidden alchemy of the moment. In certain moods, *The Hunting of the Snark* can be as consoling as *The Waste Land*.

> Erect and sublime, for one moment of time,
> In the next, that wild figure they saw
> (As if stung by a spasm) plunge into a chasm,
> While they waited and listened in awe.
>
> 'It's a Snark!' was the sound that first came to
>   their ears,
> And seemed almost too good to be true.
> Then followed a torrent of laughter and cheers:
> Then the ominous words 'It's a Boo—'
>
> Then, silence. Some fancied they heard in the air
> A weary and wandering sigh
> That sounded like '-jum!' but the others declare
> It was only a breeze that went by.
>
> They hunted till darkness came on, but they found
> Not a button, or feather, or mark,
> By which they could tell that they stood on the
>   ground
> Where the Baker had met with the Snark.

In the midst of the word he was trying to say,
In the midst of his laughter and glee,
He had softly and suddenly vanished away—
For the Snark was a Boojum, you see.

Lewis Carroll, on this reading, becomes an existential not a nonsense poet. He and his nomadic contemporary, Edward Lear, illustrate the way in which the music of words, as much as their meaning, might help us in dire straits. But this, finally, is not enough. We need Montaigne, whose conclusion becomes a spirited call to optimism.

> Let us disarm Death of his novelty and strangeness, let us converse and be familiar with him, and have nothing so frequent in our thoughts as death. Upon all occasions represent him to our imagination in his every shape; at the stumbling of a horse, at the falling of a tile, at the least prick with a pin, let us presently consider, and say to ourselves, 'Well, and what if it had been death itself?' and, thereupon, let us encourage and fortify ourselves.

Thus encouraged and fortified, we might agree that life is a risky business whose outcome is always fatal. For me, the narratives of great literature have a vital role to play in the conduct of the endgame, but we still have to concede that only the living can sustain a narrative beyond the grave.

This mundane reality becomes the meaning of mourning, and the purpose of memory. As the questions multiply, the prospect of death intensifies the enigma of living. When I started to write *Every Third Thought*, I imagined that, through the putting of words on paper, I would arrive at a conclusion, as if at a well-mapped destination.

Vain hope: in the end, questions of life, death, and consciousness baffle and defeat the search for clarification. With no possible report from beyond the grave, and no other resolution available, we are left with this one basic option: to live in the moment while the moment lasts, and to become reconciled to the acceptance of our fate. Once upon a time, writing *My Year Off* provided a kind of resolution. This time, my investigation has yielded just one intransigent outcome: that there are only more questions and an ever-deepening mystery.

To this slightly baffling challenge, the only possible rejoinder is that, as experts of the Now, we must continue to live in the present. That, after all, is the one dimension of the space-time continuum with which we have a lifetime of experience. My thoughts spin back to my schoolroom memories of reading Keats, and his reflections on mortality:

> . . . then on the shore
> Of the wide world I stand alone,
> Till Love and Fame to nothingness do sink.

'Nothingness' might turn out to be a realistic synonym for posterity. And yet, while the cerebral cortex is still firing, our vivid consciousness will continue to experience, and savour, 'the nowness of everything', Dennis Potter's inspiring phrase. But in what, during the days and weeks before death, would that 'nowness' consist? What does 'nowness' mean to me, who am conducting this investigation?

In the course of this year, ever since Prospero's words first popped into my head, Shakespeare's valedictory lines in *The Tempest* have become an ear-worm. Prospero's return to 'Milan' precedes his 'grave' – but where do I locate my own Milan, amid the turbulence of late middle age? Whenever I've described the title and subject of this book to friends and colleagues, I've elicited for myself a range of inward images for 'my Milan': a sea coast, a stretch of wild, open moorland, or a quiet patch of English countryside. My fantasy of a sequestered withdrawal from city life involves piles of books and the natural world, a library with a window on to some green shade.

These are the days that begin to chart a glide-path towards extinction. Instinctively, we hope for a soft landing, on grass, although experience suggests that the odds are against it. In truth, we are more likely to be besieged by Roth's imminent 'massacre'. Perhaps my descent has already started. As I was leaving the *Observer* offices today, I bumped into Amelia, a colleague, on her way to get a cappuccino. I asked what she was working on. 'Ageing,' she replied. 'A series.'

'Do tell me what you find out,' I said, purposely not mentioning *Every Third Thought*.

'Oh,' she replied, with the insouciance of youth. 'We're all fucked.'

As this narrative draws to its conclusion in the summer of 2016, one friend – tormented by depression

– has just committed suicide by drowning herself at dawn in the English Channel; another is dying by degrees from oesophageal cancer. Her father has just 'passed away', although with none of the serenity wrapped up in that phrase. A third . . . but I don't want to go there.

Every week brings more tales of heartbreak, and it's to this fearsome retribution that we need a riposte. Montaigne says that we should become familiar with death, which was plausible enough in the sixteenth century. But is that, however, a workable strategy in an age of death-defying medicine? Is it possible 'To begin depriving death of its greatest advantage over us'? Today, is Montaigne's exhortation feasible? 'Let us', he says, 'adopt a way clean common to the contrary one; let us deprive death of its strangeness; let us frequent it; let us get used to it; let us have nothing more often in mind than death.' Perhaps we are obliged to make the attempt. Montaigne reminds us that 'there is no place where death cannot find us – even if we constantly twist our heads about in all directions as in a suspect land.'

According to T. S. Eliot's Sweeney (in 'Fragment of an Agon'):

Birth, and copulation, and death.
That's all the facts when you come to brass tacks . . .

'In the long run, we are all dead,' says J. M. Keynes, in a notoriously controversial sentence. This stark truth does not stop those final days from being complicated or troubling. Making the best kind of exit is an art, but the years are not kind to the would-be escape artists of senescence. When Time is at war with Youth, everyone must struggle to find some kind of equipoise.

At the beginning of summer 2016, during his final weeks, I made several visits to see Matthew, an old friend, who was suffering the last stages of leukaemia in a hospice. To start with, however well-versed one might have been in Montaigne's 'frequenting' of death, there was not much sensible to say. The dying man was too much in denial about his condition, and fiercely over-committed to exercising his willpower for a short-term recovery. It would have been an act of cruelty to interrupt the comforts of his delirium.

Did his refusal to face the reality of his progressive disintegration actually help him? I debated this question with some of his circle. It was certainly his choice, but it closed down many avenues of companionship at the end. What do you say to a man in a hospice who is talking about getting better and going home next week? At the end, does it really help to 'rage against the dying of the light'?

In such circumstances, what is going to soothe those who are approaching their last exit? What story, or what words, will provide any real or serious consolation? In death, there are many competing bereavements, a continuum of loss, on all sides. There will be sadness, grief, and even agony. But is it not also possible that some will be hoping for a release? The dying have a right to their decease. In this last moment, the last gasp of 'nowness', it may be language – the thing that makes us human – that offers another kind of escape. Even paradoxical sentences can conceal paradoxical therapy.

As Shakespeare says at the end of *King Lear*, 'This is not the worst, so long as we can say "This is the worst"'.

In childhood, we repeat lines of poetry hardly knowing what they mean, and find delight in nonsense rhymes whose Zen master is Edward Lear:

> Far and few, far and few,
> Are the lands where the Jumblies live;
> Their heads are green, and their hands are blue,
> And they went to sea in a sieve.

Is it possible that, in those last moments of second childhood, there's a solace to be found in the repetition of half-remembered lines? To the insignificance of men and women at the moment where they wait – in the classical myth – on the shores of infinity can be added the idea that the heart-beat of language might be a consolation. I like to think that, approaching this rite of passage, crossing the waters of forgetfulness into the dark night of oblivion, the sharp prick of rationality might blur into a new rhythm and a new sensation that sponsors the recognition of an intervention transcending human experience. Here's more mystery. What, if anything, is there to be said about God (from whom, alas, there is no escape)?

I have a friend who jokes that she's saving up the 'three Gs' – gardening, genealogy and God – for her old age. This, I think, summarizes a fairly typical English response to issues of faith. It's here that I concede inadequacy and defeat. For better or worse, the literature devoted to questions of belief is simply too vast and too profound to be encompassed in a short book like *Every Third Thought*.

☽

With the 'dying of the light', there are some obvious and alternative responses not mentioned by Dylan Thomas. Might there not be a strange exhilaration? Or an inarticulate recognition of imminent oblivion? Or the suffering of secret grief? (I have heard tales of the terminally ill shedding tears in their comas.) For one insight into issues of belief at the moment of dying, I found myself turning to literature, to a new reading of *A Grief Observed* by C. S. Lewis.

On the face of it, this classic of bereavement describes the agony of an annihilating loss. However, as an essay-journal, *A Grief Observed* opens up many consoling avenues of inquiry into the conundrum of God's place in the wild darkness surrounding the twenty-first-century deathbed.

'Jack' Lewis had always been a man tortured by the tragedies of love, but now he was also addressing a crisis of faith. *A Grief Observed* was at first published pseudonymously. C. S. Lewis had written this little book after the death of his wife, as part of his reconciliation to her fate. A couple of years after his own death, in 1965, his estate gave permission for the book to be reissued under his own name, adding to its status as a contemporary classic.

'No one ever told me that grief felt so much like fear.' From its famous opening line, *A Grief Observed* propels its readers into an abyss of mourning. Dramatizing bereavement, it confronts the desolate survivor (representative of all readers) with an overwhelming question: 'Where is God?' Lewis's answer to this existential conundrum resonates through the rest of the book with a kind of tangible fury:

> Go to Him when your need is desperate, when all other help is vain, and what do you find? A door slammed in your face, and a sound of bolting and double-bolting on the inside. After that, silence. You may as well turn away. The longer you wait, the more emphatic the silence will become . . . What can this mean? Why is He so present a commander in our time of prosperity and so very absent a help in time of trouble?

Even a confused non-believer like me can understand the sense of betrayal. For a believer, writes Lewis, 'the conclusion I dread is not "So there's no God after all", but "So this is what God's really like. Deceive yourself no longer."' Much of his text has a self-help flavour that morphs into lyricism. There's even a suggestion that the pain associated with sorrow might be commensurate with ageing. 'Sorrow', instructs Lewis, 'turns out to be not a state but a process. It needs not a map but a history, and if I don't stop writing that history at some arbitrary point, there's no reason why I should ever stop. There is something to be chronicled every day. Grief is like a long valley, a winding valley where any bend may reveal a totally new landscape.' The same might be said of the endgame. In this context, some of Lewis's exclamations are raw and modern.

'Cancer, and cancer, and cancer,' he writes. 'My mother, my father, my wife. I wonder who is next in the queue.' Some of his best passages capture the vivid juxtaposition of consciousness and nihilism that can sometimes surround a deathbed:

> We have seen the faces of those we know best so variously, from so many angles, in so many lights, with so many expressions – waking, sleeping, laughing, crying, eating, talking, thinking – that all the impressions crowd into our memory together and cancel out in a mere blur.

This blurring of competing sensations makes *A Grief Observed* so intensely varied that it's susceptible to different readings. Above all, there's Lewis's refusal to be intimidated by death. He reports that his wife 'had lost a great deal of her old horror of it.' With this equanimity came a psychic dividend:

> When the reality came, the name [Death] and the idea were in some degree disarmed. This is important. One never meets just Cancer, or War, or Unhappiness. One only meets each hour or moment that comes. All manner of ups and downs. The thing itself [Death] is simply all these ups and downs: the rest is a name or an idea.

Another important insight is Lewis's recognition of solitude: he knows that in these dark moments, both he and she (his wife) are utterly alone. 'You can't really share someone else's weakness,' he writes, and their 'fear or pain'. Having made a ruthless analysis of the human predicament, he draws his conclusions:

> It is hard to have patience with people who say 'There is no death' or 'Death doesn't matter'. You may as well say that birth doesn't matter. I look up at the night sky. Is anything more certain than that, in all those vast times and spaces, if I were allowed to search them, I should nowhere find her face, her voice, her touch? She died. She is dead. Is the word so difficult to learn?

Lewis is at pains to express the old truth that Life is a dangerous affair. 'You will never discover how serious it was,' he writes, 'until the stakes are raised horribly high; until you find you are playing not for counters, but for every penny you have in the world.' And so, finally, Lewis articulates a story about the ordinary person's dialogue with 'God' that speaks to a secular society confronting death.

'My idea of God is not a divine idea. It has to be shattered time after time. He shatters it himself. He is the great iconoclast. Could we not almost say that this shattering is one of the marks of His presence?' Lewis's 'God' remains as capricious and fleeting as life itself ('There's always a card in his hand we didn't know about'). Wittily, he turns the idea of a 'mystery' back on humanity itself: 'Can a mortal ask questions which God finds unanswerable? Quite easily, I should think.'

I find this a provocative and appealing line of commentary. If we are going to imagine a dialogue with God, we have to be able to imagine how that might go in the delirium of the endgame. Lewis is on to this. He welcomes the irrational side of the discussion. 'All nonsense questions are unanswerable. How many hours are there in a mile? Is yellow square or round? Probably half the questions we ask . . . are like that.' On this perplexing and paradoxical note, we return to that quotidian reality, beloved of Hollywood: *No one knows anything.*

As Lewis puts it: 'The time when there is nothing at all in your soul except a cry for help may be just the time when God can't give it: you are like a drowning man who can't be helped because he clutches and grabs.' Learning not to 'clutch and grab' at explanations might be the first step towards a reconciliation with the all-important idea of acceptance.

The great song-writer Leonard Cohen was always a resonant voice of clarity, with deep inner resources of wisdom. Towards the end of 2016, shortly before he died from a fall, he discussed his future as an artist, and confided that he might never release some of the songs on which he had been working. But he was at peace with that: 'Maybe I'll get a second wind,' he told the *New Yorker*. 'I don't know. But I don't dare attach myself to a spiritual strategy. I don't dare do that. I've got some work to do. Take care of business. I am ready to die. I hope it's not too uncomfortable. That's about it for me.'

☽

In 'Sabbath', published just before his death, Oliver Sacks remains strikingly calm, writing in a kind of dream-state: 'I find my thoughts drifting to the Sabbath, and perhaps the seventh day of one's life as well, when one can feel that one's work is done, and one may, in good conscience, rest.'

Elisabeth Kübler-Ross would say that Sacks was articulating the final and valedictory stage of 'Acceptance', in which humanity becomes reconciled to its fate. This is perhaps most difficult when the world seems more than ever vivid, and alive, rich in possibilities. Sacks himself writes, 'I am now face to face with dying, but I am not finished with living.'

How to find appropriate words for this kind of reconciliation? It will not be easy. Our unquenchable instinct is to place ourselves at the centre of worldly struggles, and to exercise willpower. We are always beating back into the past, in Fitzgerald's famous words, like 'boats against the current'. Yet, at some point, humanity's instinct for self-assertion has to open a negotiation with the armies of the night.

I think, now, that we should make peace in order to be at peace. It's strange to imagine the world without our presence, and our contribution. How on earth will it survive? Behind the arrogance of this thought lurks the paradoxical truth that the only world we know is the world we have experienced, and perceived, for ourselves. 'Nowness' is the best we can hope for. This is a world that will – indeed must – die with us. While there is no satisfying conclusion, part of any ultimate reconciliation must be about coming to terms with transience and its associated mystery. Einstein once said: 'The most beautiful thing we can experience is the mysterious. It is the source of all true art and science.'

Thus the 'nowness' of things in all their mystery, properly recognized, is a necessary admission of human transience within an infinitely unfathomed universe. On this reading, mortality places mankind at the heart of a vivid but inconstant reality that is immeasurably more profound than the temporal concerns of the heroic self. This is a theme that the American novelist Marilynne Robinson has often addressed in her public utterances. Tellingly, in *The Givenness of Things*, Robinson admits how, as she approached seventy, she abruptly and inexplicably encountered a new sense of 'nowness':

> I know my life is drawing to an end. The strangeness of life on earth first of all, and then of everything that takes my attention, is very moving to me now. It feels freshly seen, like a morning that is exceptional only for the atmosphere it has of utter, unimpeachable newness, no matter how many times old Earth has tottered around the sun.

'Sometimes', concludes Robinson, 'I am so struck by an image or an idea that I cannot sleep nights.'

The sleepless mind might tell itself fearful tales in the darkness, but the mind suffused with 'nowness' creates a better narrative for the fretful self. As a non-believer, I am glad to entertain the possibility of being pleasantly surprised. I have lived with the mystery of the brain, and I think I am happy to fade into a mystery beyond the magic of the cortex. Intellectually, that seems like the best bet for the future.

20

A MONTH IN THE COUNTRY

Fear no more the heat of the sun,
Nor the furious winter's rages;
Thou thy worldly task hast done
Home art gone, and ta'en thy wages;
Golden lads and girls all must,
As chimney-sweepers, come to dust.

William Shakespeare, *Cymbeline*

Finally, it is the last day of summer, 2016. I am sitting under a tree, with a pile of books, a folder of notes, and my laptop. I have just completed a month in the country during which I've brought my story so far up to date, perhaps hoping to have negotiated some kind of private armistice with the demons of existential mystery.

I used to say that, as a stroke recoverer, I believed in celebrating normality and the active life, as far as possible. Towards the end of *My Year Off*, I even compiled a list of Dos and Don'ts. Here, at the end of *Every Third Thought*, that list has become distilled and simplified:

1. Try to keep fit
2. Accept your fate/insignificance
3. Live in the moment.

The celebration of 'nowness' must involve a rapprochement with will-power: the passivity of acceptance. I am certain that, at the end, I shall be listening not speaking; absorbing or perhaps receiving, not transmitting. When the ferryman arrives to transport me across the dark waters of the Styx, there may be no one to talk to any more, and – another 'What if?' – perhaps I shall be no longer able to speak.

At the edge of darkness, there may not be the dynamic interplay of speech and language, but – as I know from my own hospital experience – despite many other losses, there will be sound and hearing. Aural sensations are the last to fail. One of the strangest moments of my stroke, all those years ago, was lying speechless and semi-paralysed on a gurney, listening to the doctors discuss my case. I could not intervene, but I could be a spectator, and an audience, at my own descent into the underworld, that inevitable screening of the endgame.

To me, *Every Third Thought* suggests that the mystery of death and dying is only equalled by the mystery of life and living. Another conclusion: happy endings will be fortuitous. Consoling narratives must be patched together from transient fragments of experience.

So I wrap this up with some simple questions for this new century. Why not celebrate 'nowness'? Discover the joy of wisdom and experience. Cherish your family. Celebrate the human drama in all its variety. Be happy to be old. Feast on the marrow of life while you can. Pass on to fellow-survivors, friends, and family a positive delight in the world. Even tormented old John Donne in his *Devotions* seems to find cause for optimism:

> No man is well that understands not, that values not, his well-being, that hath not a cheerfulness and a joy in it; and whosoever hath this joy hath a desire to communicate, to propagate, that which occasions his happiness and joy to others.

In truth, there is no other sensible narrative available. Unless you believe in an afterlife – which I don't – this must be the only way forward. It may be a hard lesson but, as Flaubert pragmatically once observed, 'Everything must be learned, from reading to dying.' On the other hand, there are also the mysterious revolutions of luck, the wheel of chance – and thereby hangs a tale. This is where I close, with a new and unexpected kind of love-story.

☽

We met under a crab-apple tree, just outside Salisbury, in the garden of some mutual friends, during a summer lunch party.

It was a long time ago: about ten years.

I was contentedly married to Sarah, going full tilt with family life. Alice and Isobel, who can't have been much more than nine and seven, respectively, were tearing up and down the grass with their friends, the triplets, who would soon take them across the meadow next door to swim stark naked in the cool river that prattled away in the distance, beyond a hayfield and a yurt.

And there I was, sitting at a garden table, watching these tiny riots of childhood breaking out around me when this rather elfin, smiling woman, almost 'a girl' (the word she would shortly use to describe the other mums on the grass), came up to say hello. She had just read *My Year Off*. Her mother was recovering from a stroke, she said, with swift, disarming candour. Perhaps we could talk?

What did I say, and what did we discuss? I have no memory, but I cannot forget the sensations of that conversation with Emma – she had introduced herself very easily as she sat down opposite me at the table.

I remember the sunshine bursting round us through the green web of overhanging branches. I think I remember drinking rosé, and feeling stunned and slightly exhilarated by Emma's effortless and gracious manner.

We were talking about matters of life and death, and she was mixing gravity with laughter in the most infectious way, drawing me out, and opening me up with a deft sequence of highly personal questions about the aftermath of my 'brain attack'.

I have never minded sharing the experience of my stroke, but this was more than sharing. This was in danger of becoming self-revelation. I remember thinking: I will tell you everything. Ask me any question, and I'll answer, yes and yes, I will . . . Oh, whistle and I'll come to you.

And so we talked. Picnic plates came and went; drinks were filled and refilled. Sarah must have been somewhere with our friends, or attending to the girls.

In truth, I was oblivious. What had begun as the kind of conversation often sponsored by the afterlife of *My Year Off*, had become something quite different. Strangely, it didn't seem like a reckless flirtation. It felt quite natural; a conversation with an old friend. Such an old friend, apparently, that she did not feel the need to say goodbye.

At some point, distracted by the children, I turned round to discover that Emma had vanished as silently as she had appeared, in a way that I now know to be characteristic. I recall wondering if I should ask our hostess about this mysterious guest, but thought better of it: Don't go there.

Lunch ended; the long summer's day faded into twilight; we all piled into family cars to go home, and everyday life filled the void once more.

☽

Ten years passed. Everyday life turned cold and bitter. I cannot explain the sad end of my marriage to Sarah except to confess that our love died, for no obvious reason, a painful admission. A break-up is like a death in the family. We went through the stages of Denial, Anger, Bargaining, Depression, and finally Acceptance (yes, there was counselling: a fruitless attempt to scramble into a lifeboat long after the ship had gone down). Somehow, we survived, salvaging scraps of parental continuity and coherence from the wreckage of family life in London and New York.

I had always known that the life of the stroke survivor is often cursed by divorce and depression. To begin with, I believed I had somehow escaped these furies. But now the professional frustrations of mid-life, mixed with the rallentando of getting on in years, contributed to an overwhelming sense of decline and failure. Sarah's departure for her former New York home in July 2013, the month of my sixteenth birthday, seemed to set the seal on a vicious downward spiral in my life-cycle. The third act that beckoned hardly seemed to be an enticing prospect.

☽

Alone in a new flat in West London, I began to negotiate an uncertain way forward as a single man. Solitude has its attractions, especially after the catastrophe of a failed marriage. Having time to read and reflect, to re-evaluate the important parts of my life and career, was quite appealing. We all need a room of our own.

At the same time, while the security of my bachelor apartment was a liberation, it was also a prison. I was lonely. In darker moments, I imagined that it would be my fate to be ageing and solitary for years to come. In this defeated mood, I was grateful for any distraction and quickly came to accept weekend invitations.

In retrospect, I was too numb with sadness to understand what was happening. At that moment, but not for much longer, I was going through the everyday routines like a Robinson Crusoe, though, unlike Crusoe, bereft of optimism, burdened with low-grade dissatisfaction bordering on despair, and hardly daring to look into the future. Single friends, who understood how to navigate this stage of life, had advised me to book up my weekends, and to make good plans for Christmas. I understood that they were right, but had so far done precisely nothing about it.

☽

But then, in the autumn of 2013, about three months after Sarah's departure, my friends, the —s, under whose crab-apple tree I had conversed with Emma all those years before, suggested a weekend in Dorset at the beginning of November. Why not? Better start somewhere.

As the date approached, I found a message on my mobile: could I give one of their weekend guests a lift?

I thought no more about it, conducted a brief exchange of texts about a possible departure time and suitable rendezvous, and answered the buzzer in my flat late on a Friday afternoon with only the most fleeting speculation about my passenger, a woman whose unfamiliar name had become attached to an anonymous mobile-phone number.

I took the lift down to the gloomy hallway, and hurried into the street through the heavy glass doors of the apartment block in which I was now living. Outside, it was cold and grey, with imminent autumn rain. There was, apparently, no one waiting. I turned to look round, glancing down the pavement. This was the moment – a scene from an improbably romantic movie – I will never forget.

Standing there, with a single suitcase, beneath her umbrella, slight and solitary and self-possessed, was the girl from the crab-apple tree. 'Hi,' said Emma, lighting up with her lovely, heartbreaking smile. 'Haven't we met before?'

THE END

Bibliography

Al Alvarez: *The Savage God: A Study of Suicide* (London, 1971)

Martin Amis: *Experience* (London, 2000)

Julian Barnes: *Nothing To Be Frightened Of* (London, 2008)

John Bayley: *Iris: A Memoir of Iris Murdoch* (London, 1998)

Peter Bazalgette: *The Empathy Instinct* (London, 2017)

Paul Bloom: *Against Empathy* (London, 2017)

Ronald Blythe: *The View in Winter: Reflections on Old Age* (London, 1979)

Joan Didion: *The Year of Magical Thinking* (New York, 2005)

Jenni Diski: *In Gratitude* (London, 2016)

Norman Doidge: *The Brain that Changes Itself* (London, 2007)

John Donne: *Devotions Upon Emergent Occasions* (1624)

Barbara Ehrenreich: *Smile or Die: How Positive Thinking Fooled America and the World* (New York, 2009)

Nora Ephron: *I Feel Bad About My Neck: And Other Thoughts About Being a Woman* (New York, 2006)

Erik Erikson: *Identity: Youth and Crisis* (New York, 1968)

Simon Gray: *The Complete Smoking Diaries* (London, 2013)

Christopher Hitchens: *Mortality* (London, 2012)

Siri Hustvedt: *A Woman Looking At Men Looking at Women: Essays on Art, Sex, and the Mind* (London, 2016)

Deborah Hutton: *What Can I Do to Help: 75 Practical Ideas for Family and Friends from Cancer's Frontline* (London, 2005)

Joseph Jebelli: *In Pursuit of Memory: The Fight Against Alzheimer's* (London, 2017)

Paul Kalanithi: *When Breath Becomes Air* (New York, 2016)

Michael Kinsley: *Old Age: A Beginner's Guide* (New York, 2016)

Elisabeth Kübler-Ross: *On Death and Dying* (London, 1970)

Christopher Lasch: *The Culture of Narcissism: American Life in an Age of Diminishing Expectations* (New York, 1979)

Andrew Lees: *Mentored by a Madman: The William Burroughs Experiment* (London, 2016)

C. S. Lewis: *A Grief Observed* (London, 1961)

Sarah Lyall: *The Anglo Files: A Field Guide to the British* (New York, 2008)

Robert McCrum: *My Year Off* (London, 1998)

Henry Marsh: *Do No Harm: Stories of Life, Death and Brain Surgery* (London, 2014)

Sherwin Nuland: *How We Die* (New York, 1993)

Adam Phillips: *Darwin's Worms* (London, 1999)

Max Porter: *Grief is the Thing with Feathers* (London, 2015)

Terry Pratchett: *A Slip of the Keyboard: Collected Non-Fiction* (London, 2013)

Katie Roiphe: *The Violet Hour: Great Writers at the End* (London, 2016)

Oliver Sacks: *Awakenings* (London, 1973)

Julia Samuel: *Grief Works* (London, 2017)

Muriel Spark: *Memento Mori* (London, 1959).

Raymond Tallis: *The Black Mirror: Fragments of an Obituary for Life* (London, 2015)

Des Wilson: *Growing Old: The Last Campaign* (London, 2014)

Chapter Notes

1. A Matter of Life and Death

4 'Now we are living in hell': quoted in *My Year Off*, p. xvii.

6 'This is not going to end well': interview, *Scotsman*, 7 February 2010.

8 Empathy might be one key: see Peter Bazalgette, *The Empathy Instinct* (London, 2017) and Paul Bloom, *Against Empathy* (London, 2017).

9 'it's sad to be over sixty': Nora Ephron, 'Considering the Alternative', in *I Feel Bad About My Neck*, p. 198.

9 'Never send to know': John Donne, *Devotions Upon Emergent Occasions* (1624).

2. Injury Time

11 Among older people: Atul Gawande, *Being Mortal* (London, 2014), p. 40.

14 'Well? Shall we go?': Samuel Beckett, *Waiting for Godot* (London, 1956), pp. 54 and 94.

15 'In the meantime, let us try and converse': ibid, p. 62.

16 'That's man all over for you': ibid, p. 11.

16 what Beckett calls 'failing better': The full quotation, from *Worstward Ho*, is: 'Nothing else ever. Ever tried. Ever failed. No matter. Try again. Fail again. Fail better.'

18 'Thus bad begins, and worse': *Hamlet*, 3, iv, 181.

18 'We have time to grow old': Samuel Beckett, *Waiting for Godot*. p. 91.

19 'Go quick away': *The Tempest*, 5, i, 339–46.

3. Forever Young?

20 'The days of our years': Psalms 90: 10.

21 'The path forward would seem obvious': Paul Kalanithi, 'How Long Have I Got Left?', *New York Times*, 25 January 2014.

22 'the whirligig of time': *Twelfth Night*, 5, i, 309.

28 'Considering the alternative': Nora Ephron, *I Feel Bad About My Neck*, pp. 202–3.

4. I–Me–Mine

31 The lines of power: Atul Gawande, *Being Mortal* (London, 2014), p. 22.

32 The seventh-best selling book of all time: more than fifty million copies in print in almost fifty different countries.

33 'We are a generation': Nora Ephron: *I Feel Bad About My Neck*, p. 201.

37 'There is a world elsewhere': *Coriolanus*, 3, iii, 139.

38 'We study health': John Donne, *Devotions Upon Emergent Occasions* (1624): 'The first Alteration, the First Grudging, of the Sickness', Meditation 1.

40 The discovery that the brain: see 'Brain survivors',
    Guardian, 4 June 2015.

43 In new stroke units, across Britain: see Robert
    McCrum, 'Twenty Years in Search of the Stroke
    Detector', *Observer*, 22 January 2017.

5. The Skull of Man

46 'A landscape opened up before me': 'The Terrible
    Beauty of Brain Surgery', Karl Ove Knausgaard,
    New York Times, 30 December 2015.

48 atoms in the brain: Richard Feynman, *What Do You
    Care What Other People Think?* (New York, 2001),
    p. 244, quoted in Marilynne Robinson, *The
    Givenness of Things* (London, 2015), p. 262.

49 'the hard problem': Various cognitive scientists claim
    authorship of 'the hard problem', an expression that
    passed into the mainstream when Tom Stoppard
    adopted it as the title for a new play in 2014. The
    strongest claim comes from David Chalmers, the
    Australian philosopher who coined the phrase in
    1995.

49 The tantalizing frontier: Ana Perez Galvan. She
    writes 'I googled the ICTUS definition and the entry
    that comes out in Spanish for it when you type
    ICTUS is in fact this one. https://es.wikipedia.org/
    wiki/Accidente_cerebrovascular.' Ana adds that 'The
    names *cerebrovascular accident, brain damage, brain
    hemorrage* or the lesser used name *apoplexy* are used
    as synonyms of the word ictus'. There isn't an entry
    in Wikipedia for 'ictus' as such. Email 4 March
    2016.

51 Life expectancy continues: In 1950, children under the age of five amounted to approximately 10 per cent of the US and UK population, while the population over eighty years old numbered about 1 per cent.

51 cut their own toenails: Des Wilson: *Growing Old* (London, 2014), p. 39.

51 The predictions suggest: Atul Gawande, *Being Mortal* (London, 2014), p. 36.

51 Since 1950, the median age: see David Willetts, *The Pinch: How the Baby Boomers Took Their Children's Future* (London, 2010).

52 three main suspects: Sherwin B. Nuland, *How We Die* (New York, 1993).

52 In May 2016, the BBC reported: 'Too many delay seeking dementia diagnosis, charity says', available at http://www.bbc.co.uk/news/health-36286016.

6. Silly of Me

54 'The Question therefore was not whether a Man': Jonathan Swift, *Gulliver's Travels* (World's Classics, Oxford, 1986), p. 197.

55 the novelist Stephen King: *New York Times*, 31 October 2015.

56 When, at the age of fifty-eight: Julian Barnes, *Nothing To Be Frightened Of*, p. 97.

56 'O let me not be mad, not mad, sweet heaven!': *King Lear*, 1, v, 42–3.

57 'Our basest beggars': These quotations from *King Lear* are taken from 2, iv, 259–81.

58 'Let me have surgeons': *King Lear*, 4, vi, 194–5.

58 'You must bear with me': *King Lear*, 4, vii, 84.

58 'I'm sixty. That's supposed to be': Terry Pratchett, *A Slip of the Keyboard*, p. 311.

59 'something was going wrong': ibid., pp. 312–13.

59 'know anyone who has got better': ibid., pp. 305–10.

59 'I can still work at home': ibid., p. 306.

60 'It is a strange life': ibid., p. 316.

61 'never amuse themselves with reading': Jonathan Swift, *Gulliver's Travels*, p. 198.

61 Prunella Scales is a much-loved: *The Times*, 10 December 2015.

62 'It seems to me': Pratchett, *A Slip of the Keyboard*, p. 327.

7. Losing the Plot

63 William Burroughs' experiments: see A. J. Lees, *Mentored by a Madman*, pp. 1–27.

64 'I would always encourage stem-cell': interview with Professor Andrew Lees, 11 April 2016.

64 'The name of the author': Billy Collins, 'Forgetfulness'.

65 'poised to become the second leading cause': Joseph Jebelli, *In Pursuit of Memory: The Fight Against Alzheimer's* (London, 2017), p. xi. 'We're at the point,' writes Jebelli, 'at which almost everyone knows someone – a family member or friend – who has been affected.'

65 Six million inhabitants: Michael Brooks, *New Statesman*, 30 June 2016.

67 Alzheimer's is everywhere: In late 2015, the BBC

actually reported on a possible 'cure' for Alzheimer's. Researchers at the University of Southampton had posted findings that supported the evidence that inflammation in the brain is what drives the disease. A drug used to block the production of immune cells called microglia cells in the brains of mice had been found to have a positive effect. Up until then, most drugs used to treat dementia had targeted amyloid plaques in the brain. The study, published in the journal *Brain*, suggested that targeting inflammation in the brain, caused by a build-up of microglia, could halt progression of the disease. At the moment of writing, however, this 'breakthrough' is still undergoing further analysis.

67 a recent issue of the magazine *Brain*: January 2016.

68 inspired by Burroughs: 'Apomorphine,' he wrote later, 'acts on the back brain to normalize the bloodstream in such a way that the enzyme system of addiction is destroyed.'

68 this was the focus: see Robert McCrum on Lees and Burroughs, *Observer*, 26 October 2014. See also Lees, *Mentored by a Madman*.

69 Once the difficult diagnosis: Andrew Lees, *Alzheimer's: The Silent Plague* (London, 2012), p. 13.

70 The poet W. H. Auden once compared: Auden's line is persistently misquoted. It first occurs in 'Marginalia' in 1965, where the poet writes about the 'thought of his own death / Like the distant roll of thunder at a picnic.'

72 Her husband, John Bayley, reported: see John Bayley, *Iris*, p. 41.

73 Bayley recalls 'a brisk exchange': ibid., p. 53.

73 'Our mode of communication': ibid., p. 70.

74 'Dressing most days': ibid., p. 81.

74 'Most days are in fact': ibid., p. 58.

75 'I made a savage comment': ibid., p. 249.

75 'The exasperation of being followed': ibid., p. 255.

75 'The words which Iris used': ibid., p. 277.

76 'What will [Iris] do': ibid., p. 274.

76 'When former US president': Lees, *Alzhiemer's*, p. 17.

8. Do No Harm

80 'How does it feel', he asks: Henry Marsh, *Do No Harm*, p. ix.

80 'Much of what happens in hospitals': ibid., p. 3.

85 'It's been a wonderful life': ibid., p. 199.

87 he likes to quote René Leriche: ibid., p. 5.

88 'I may very well have to go through a time': In *Do No Harm*, Marsh also writes, 'I must hope that I live my life now in such a way that, like my mother, I will be able to die without regret', p. 199.

88 Marsh knows what dying can mean: Henry Marsh, *Do No Harm*, p. 198.

89 As *Sickness* is the greatest misery: John Donne, *Devotions Upon Emergent Occasions*, Meditation V.

9. Astride of a Grave

91 One serving nurse: comments added to *Merriam Webster*'s online edition.

91 etymology provides a helpful corrective: *Merriam Webster*, online.

92 'One day he went dumb': Samuel Beckett, *Waiting for Godot*, p. 89.

92 The 'sleeping sickness' pandemic of 1916–17: Oliver Sacks, *Awakenings*, pp. xxvi–xxxviii.

92 a kaleidoscope of bizarre: Lees, op. cit., p. 52.

10. The Will to Live

97 'People's capacity to survive': Phillips, op. cit., p. 115.

98 one every ten minutes: In the UK, twelve thousand will die from breast cancer every year.

100 Kate heard from a close friend: IORT is still in the trial stage, and is awaiting approval from NICE (the National Institute for Health and Care Excellence).

11. The Person Who Was Ill

117 'the commonest neurological cause': Andrew Lees, *Alzheimer's* (London, 2012), p. 24.

12. Where Are We Going?

120 It was in 1817 that Dr James Parkinson: see Sacks, *Awakenings*, p. 3. See also Andrew Lees, *Alzheimer's* (London, 2012).

121 For Max, his diagnosis of Parkinson's: for a witty, personal account of the disease, see Michael Kinsley, *Old Age: A Beginner's Guide* (New York, 2016).

126 Van Gogh's three questions: *1897*, Paul Gauguin, Museum of Fine Arts, Boston.

129 'Grief turns out to be a place': Joan Didion, *The Year of Magical Thinking*, p. 188.

129 'Words have a longevity': Paul Kalanithi: *When Breath Becomes Air*, p. 53.

13. The Good Death

134 'Be absolute for death': *Measure for Measure*, 3, i, 4–5.

134 'We defy augury': *Hamlet*, 5, ii, 218–22.

136 Tolstoy's novella: Leo Tolstoy: *The Death of Ivan Ilych*, translated by Aylmer and Louise Maude (OUP, 1935). I have taken all quoted extracts from this edition.

136 Russian writers doing things: see Leo Tolstoy, *The Death of Ivan Ilych*, translated by Aylmer and Louise Maude.

138 'Everyone owes nature a death': see Katie Roiphe, *The Violet Hour*. I have drawn freely on her account of Freud's last days.

14. The Necessity of Dying

145 'I can remember being in Bristol': Phillips has given another account of this phase to the *Paris Review*, 'The Art of Non-fiction', no. 7, issue 208, Spring 2014. 'When I was seventeen, I read Carl Jung's *Memories, Dreams, Reflections*, and I thought it was an interesting, exciting life. And then I read D.W. Winnicott's *Playing and Reality* when it came out, and I had a tremendous feeling of affinity for the book. I don't exactly know what I thought of it – I can't remember exactly – but I felt that I completely understood it, and I knew then that I wanted to be

a child psychotherapist.' (Interview with Paul Holdengräber).

145 'When I started in psychoanalysis': *Paris Review*, 2014.

146 It's time to talk about what Freud: 'We must make friends with the necessity of dying'. Freud, S. (1913). [SEL289a1] The Theme of the Three Caskets. *The Standard Edition of the Complete Psychological Works of Sigmund Freud*, Volume XII (1911–1913): *The Case of Schreber, Papers on Technique and Other Works*, pp. 289–302 edited by James Strachey. Collected Papers, 4 (London, Hogarth Press, 1925).

150 This is a response echoed by the American playwright Wallace Shawn: *Guardian*, 26 November 2015.

151 'We've begun rejecting the institutionalized': Gawande op. cit., p. 93.

151 'People's capacity to survive': see Adam Phillips, *Darwin's Worms*, p. 115–16.

154 '[They] thought of themselves as trying to tell': ibid., p. 11.

154 Phillips goes on to quote Wallace Stevens: op. cit., p. 12.

15. Last Words

157 'It is profoundly interesting to know': quoted in Gordon Bowker, *George Orwell* (London, 2003), p. 413.

157 'It would be hard to pin down': Katie Roiphe, op. cit., p. 8.

158 'He parted just between twelve and one': William

Shakespeare: *Henry the Fifth*, Act II, scene 3. There are differing versions of this speech, derived from differing, and often corrupt, Quarto and Folio editions.

159 On learning that he was mortally ill: Hume's memoir is cited in Oliver Sacks, *Gratitude* (London, 2015), pp 16–17.

159 Boswell's report of that last meeting: see *The Private Papers of James Boswell*, Geoffrey Scott and Frederick A. Pottle, eds. (London and New York, 1951), vol. 12, pp. 227–32.

164 'And now, weak, short of breath': Oliver Sacks, *Gratitude*, p. 45.

169 'If it were a race': Jenni Diski, *In Gratitude*, p. 156.

16. One Foot In The Grave

176 'What is it worth, then': from 'Event Horizon', *Sentenced to Life* (London, 2015).

179 to recite some of Catullus: I am grateful to Nigel Williams for his free translation of 'Carmen 101'.

I've flown, my brother, to this wretched thing
Your funeral, where I'm supposed to give
Some useless compliments to your dumb dust
That foul disease has taken you from me.
Oh my unhappy brother – it's not fair –
But I must, in the meantime, pay my dues
As we did for our parents when they died.
So, take my tears, that fall and will not dry
In everlasting greeting and goodbye.

17. Staring at the Sun

183 'There is nothing you can do': Nora Ephron, *I Feel Bad About My Neck*, p. 202.

183 'Finally, a good plot': I am advised by David Benedict that many have claimed this gag. Most plausible was Larry Gelbart – co-author of *A funny Thing Happened on the Way to the Forum*, and the producer/creator of *M*A*S*H*. He also wrote *Tootsie*.

183 'My father spent': Jon Henley, the *Guardian*, 3 February 2016.

188 'Death doesn't really feel eventual': Ephron, op. cit., p. 205.

18. The Dying of the Light

196 'The common people are not stupid': Pratchett: op. cit., pp. 359–61.

197 'The stoppage of circulation': Sherwin Nuland, *How We Die* (New York, 1993), p. xviii.

197 'Dying – the fact of death': see also Christopher Isherwood, *A Single Man* (London, 1964), pp. 151–52.

200 'If I were a writer of books': (Michael Screech, trans.) – Michel de Montaigne: *The Complete Essays* (London: Allen Lane, The Penguin Press, 1991), p. 87.

201 'Our culture is imbued': Julia Samuel, *Grief Works* (London, 2017), p. 45.

19. The Nowness of Everything

204 readers get a thrill from the special: see Blake
Morrison, 'Too much information?', *Guardian*,
27 November 2015.

206 'Let us disarm Death': Screech, op. cit., p. 92.

212 'No one ever told me': Lewis, *A Grief Observed*
(London, 1962). All subsequent quotations are from
the Faber & Faber 'Readers Edition', 2015.

217 'I find my thoughts drifting': Sacks, *Gratitude*
(London, 2015), p. 15.

218 'I know my life is drawing': Marilynne Robinson,
The Givenness of Things (London, 2015) p. 218.

20. A Month in the Country

219 'Fear no more': *Cymbeline*, 4, ii, 258–63.

219 Towards the end of: *My Year Off* (3rd edition,
2015), p. 240.

221 'No man is well that understands': John Donne,
Devotions, Meditation 8, 'The King sends his own
physician'.

223 'Ten years passed': Elisabeth Kübler-Ross: *On Death
and Dying* (London, 1970).

Acknowledgements

A special thanks to various friends who provided invaluable comments, criticisms and insights at different stages of composition: Peter Bazalgette, Margy Bearn, Denys Blakeway, Hilary Boyd, Don and Cressida Connolly, William Cran, John-Paul Davidson, Charles Elton, Emma Fane, Melissa Fitzgerald, Elizabeth Frayling-Cork, Ana Perez Galvan, Malcolm Gladwell, Siri Hustvedt, Clive James, Sara Kestelman, Kirsty Lang, Christine McCrum, Henry Marsh, Adam Phillips, Jonathan Powell, Jim Smith, Salley Vickers, and, as ever, my old friend Nigel Williams.

For years, that maestro of all-round fitness Dreas Reyneke has provided a rare and exceptional mix of physical and mental consolation. My dramatic departure from his exercise studio in June 2014 provided the occasion for the start of this story. Without him, in so many ways, *Every Third Thought* could not have been written.

After Dreas, in the department of *bien-être*, sincere thanks are due to Simon Bryer for his devoted attention, and also to Susanna Chancellor for providing the perfect Umbrian sanctuary in which to complete this book.

At my newspaper the *Observer*, a special salute goes to

my nearest colleagues Vanessa Thorpe and Paul Webster, as well as to our editor John Mulholland.

At ICM, I must thank my agent Amanda Urban; at Curtis Brown, Jonathan Lloyd; and, at Picador, my indefatigable editor Sophie Jonathan who first recognized that *My Year Off* was not the last word on the story of my ill-health.

From among the medical profession, I owe a special debt of gratitude to Richard Greenwood, Neil Kitchen, Martin Koltzenburg, Andrew Lees, Lynn Morgan, and Nick Ward.

I must also single out for special thanks Ben Macintyre, his pioneering Achaglachgach Writers' Colony and its remarkable team of trustees: Charles Cumming, Blanche Girouard, Kate Hubbard, Clare Longrigg, Magnus Macintyre, Natalia Naish, and Roland Phillips.

Finally, a heart-felt thank you to Sarah Lyall; and also to our daughters Alice and Isobel to whom these words are dedicated with my love, as ever.

Permissions

'At my father's bedside, I learned what death looks like' was originally printed in the *Guardian* on 3rd February 2016, and is extracted with permission from Guardian News and Media and Jon Henley.

Lines from 'Balcony Scene', 'Event Horizon', and 'Sunset Hails a Rising' by Clive James are from *Sentenced to Life*, Picador, 2015, copyright © Clive James 2015.

Lines from Dylan Thomas's poem 'Do Not Go Gentle into That Good Night' appear here with permission from the author's representatives. By Dylan Thomas, from *The Poems of Dylan Thomas*, copyright © 1952 by Dylan Thomas. Reprinted by permission of New Directions Publishing Corp.

Lines from 'Forgetfulness' by Billy Collins are from *Questions About Angels*, University of Pittsburgh Press, 1999, copyright © Billy Collins 1991.

Lines from 'Fragment of an Agon' are from *Sweeney Agonistes – Fragments of an Aristophanic Melodrama* by T. S. Eliot (Faber and Faber, 1932).

Lyrics from 'I Me Mine' by George Harrison are copyright © Harrisongs Ltd, 1970.

Excerpt from *Murphy*, copyright © 1938 by the Estate of Samuel Beckett. Used by permission of Grove/Atlantic, Inc. Any third party use of this material, outside of this publication, is prohibited.

Excerpt from *On Death and Dying* by Elizabeth Kübler-Ross (Routledge, 2009) is copyright © Elizabeth Kübler-Ross 1969.

The obituary from the *Saco Times* was published in *Portland Press Herald/Maine Sunday Telegram* from 22 December to 23 December 2015.

Excerpts from *Waiting For Godot* copyright © 1954 by Grove Press, Inc.; Copyright © renewed 1982 by Samuel Beckett. Used by permission of Grove/Atlantic, Inc. Any third party use of this material, outside of this publication, is prohibited.